Project Management Practitioner's Handbook

Project Management Practitioner's Handbook

Ralph L. Kliem
Irwin S. Ludin

AMACOM

American Management Association

New York • Atlanta • Boston • Chicago • Kansas City • San Francisco • Washington, D.C.
Brussels • Mexico City • Tokyo • Toronto

*This book is available at a special
discount when ordered in bulk quantities.
For information, contact Special Sales Department,
AMACOM, a division of American Management Association,
1601 Broadway, New York, NY 10019.*

Library of Congress Cataloging-in-Publication Data

Kliem, Ralph L.
  *Project management practioner's handbook / Ralph L. Kliem, Irwin
S. Ludin.*
      p. cm.
  Includes bibliographical references and index.
  ISBN 0-8144-0396-4
  1. Industrial project management. I. Ludin, Irwin S. II. Title.
HD69.P75K594   1998
  658.4'04—DC21   *98-22616*
                                                                     CIP

Printing number

  10 9 8 7 6 5 4 3 2 1

Contents

Preface

Well into the swiftly approaching millennium, project management will continue to be a highly desired skill in the midst of great change. Because rigid organizational boundaries and responsibilities have blurred and new technologies are changing the ways of doing business, results must be delivered more quickly and accurately than ever before. These circumstances call for people who can deal with ambiguity and time pressures while simultaneously accomplishing project goals—in other words, people who display excellence in project management.

In this book, we present the route to achieving the knowledge and expertise that will help you display excellence in project management, on any type of project in any industry. Using a wedding-business case study, we present the basic principles, tools, and techniques so that readers can easily understand and apply the material.

Starting with Chapter 2, you'll learn the six basic functions of project management. You'll learn how to:

1. *Lead* a project throughout its cycle; it's so important that it is the first topic.
2. *Define* a project's goals and objectives so everyone agrees on the results and knows success when they see it.
3. *Plan* a project in a way that results in a road map that people will confidently follow, not just the project manager.
4. *Organize* a project in a manner that increases the efficiency and effectiveness of the team, resulting in greater productivity.
5. *Control* a project so that its momentum and direction are not overtaken by "scope creep."
6. *Close* a project in a manner so that it lands smoothly rather than crashes.

The book comprises three major parts. Part I establishes the fundamentals of project management, with an overview of the field today, provides information on the wedding case study, and provides a general look at what constitutes leadership. Part II is the heart of the volume, with chapters covering the key issues that face project managers today. Based on the six functions just listed, these chapters discuss setting up your project structure, assessing its progress, and achieving its goals. We cover such topics as working with new teaming structures and styles, motivating people, estimating costs, and dealing with change. At the end of each chapter is a series of questions that will help you apply your new knowledge to an existing or upcoming project.

Part III contains additional tips, such as how to work with new technologies and how to manage or decrease risk. The Appendix material refers to the case study, the Glossary is a quick reference to special terms, and the References are suggestions for further reading.

The authors have applied the principles, tools, and techniques in this book successfully in a wide variety of projects: audit, construction, documentation, engineering, information systems, insurance, manufacturing, support services/help desk, and telecommunications projects, as well as in other environments. The book is based on our combined experience of more than fifty years in business management, operations, and information systems. As the founders and executives of the consulting firm Practical Creative Solutions, Inc., of Redmond, Washington, we offer products, services, and training programs designed to meet the special needs of our varied clients.

Project management works—if you know what it is and how to do it. After reading this book, you will be able to join the ranks of effective and successful project managers.

Project Management Practitioner's Handbook

Part I

An Overview of Projects and Their Effective and Successful Management

Chapter 1

Project Management in Today's World of Business

The project manager has never had a tougher job. Companies are always in transition now, remodeling and reorganizing to meet the latest global challenges. Competition is keen and only the flexible will survive. These business conditions translate directly to the greater demands for efficient, effective management of an entire spectrum of projects.

For example, a rise in use of distributed systems technology (e.g., client/server, Intranet, and Internet computing) and telecommuting has accelerated the disappearance of organizational boundaries and hierarchical management levels. Along with this blurring of organizational levels has come employee empowerment. Many companies now grant employees greater responsibilities and decision-making authority (e.g., self-directed work teams).

And the changes just don't stop. Many companies view projects as investments, integral parts of their strategic plans. This means the project managers must continually demonstrate their contribution to the bottom line. With this alliance between strategic plan and project management comes an increasingly close but often tense relationship between project and process management. Contrary to popular belief, project management and process management *are* compatible; projects become integral players in using and implementing processes. But failure to effectively manage a key project could cause a malfunction in the core process! This relationship between process and project management also manifests itself in a need to integrate multiple projects when they involve common core processes, thus requiring even greater integration to ensure such processes are not adversely affected.

The nature of today's workforce has changed in many companies. Employees are no longer offered or seek long-term employment—many people and companies want flexibility or mobility. Such changes add a new dimension to the work being done on a project—a dimension that directly affects relationships and ways of doing business. And many projects now involve people from different occupations and backgrounds. The globalization of the nation's business, for instance, requires that a project manager's skills go beyond being able to put together a flowchart.

As the economy continues to expand, key resources will become limited and project managers will need alternative ways to obtain expertise, such as by using consultants and outsourcing. Certainly, project managers in the past have faced similar problems of providing alternative sources of expertise—but never on as great a scale as they do today.

Market pressures complicate the management of projects, too. Customers not only want a quality product but also want it sooner. Time-to-market pressures force project managers to be efficient and effective to an unprecedented degree. The complexity involved in managing projects has never been greater and will likely only grow in the future. So, too, will the risks for failure. It is more critical than ever that the pieces of the project be in place to ensure delivery of the final service on time and within budget and to guarantee that it be of the highest quality.

Tom Peters, the great management consultant, was correct when he said that project management is the skill of the 1990s. But it is the skill of the future as well. The need for managing projects efficiently and effectively has never been greater and so are the rewards for its success. But having good project management practices in place will no longer suffice; what is required now is excellence in project management if project success is to be the norm.

PROJECT MANAGEMENT DEFINED

Despite a changing project environment, the fundamental tools of project management remain the same regardless of project or industry. For example, managing a marketing project requires the same skills as managing a software engineering project.

But what is a project? What is project management? A *project* is a discrete set of activities performed in a logical sequence to attain a specific result. Each activity, and the entire project, has a start and stop date. *Project management* is the tools, techniques, and processes for defining, planning, organizing, controlling, and leading a project as it completes its tasks and delivers the results. But let's take a closer look at the functions of project management just mentioned.

■ *Lead*　To inspire the participants to accomplish the goals and objectives at a level that meets or exceeds expectations. It is the only function of project management that occurs simultaneously with the other functions. Whether defining, planning, organizing, or controling, the project manager uses leadership to execute the project efficiently and effectively.

Introducing Project Management

The top management in some companies does not understand that project management is what is needed. How do you convince people that project management will help them?

Introducing project management is a change management issue, even a paradigm shift. That's because project management disciplines will affect many policies, procedures, and processes. They will also affect technical, operational, economic, and human resources issues. Such changes can be dramatic, and many people—as in many change efforts—will resist or embrace change, depending on how it is perceived.

Here are some steps for introducing project management within an organization.

1. Build an awareness of project management. You can distribute articles and books on the subject and attend meetings sponsored by the Project Management Institute and the American Management Association.

2. Establish a need for project management. Identify opportunities for applying project management, particularly as a way to solve problems. Collect data on previous project performance and show statistically and anecdotally how project management would have improved results.

3. Benchmark. You can compare your organization's experience with projects to that of companies that have used project management.

4. Find a sponsor. No matter what case you can make for project management, you still need someone with enough clout to support its introduction.

5. Select a good pilot. Avoid taking on too much when introducing the idea of project management. Select a project that's not too visible but also one that people care about. The project serves as a proving ground for your new ideas.

6. Communicate the results. As the project progresses, let management know about its successes and failures. Profile the project as a "lessons learned" experience.

7. Provide consultation on other projects. With the expertise acquired on your pilot project, apply your knowledge to other projects. Your advice will enable others to see the value of project management.

▪ *Define*   To determine the overall vision, goals, objectives, scope, responsibilities, and deliverables of a project. A common way to capture this information is with a statement of work. This is a document that delineates the above information and is signed by all interested parties.

▪ *Plan*   To determine the steps needed to execute a project, assign who will perform them, and identify their start and completion dates. Planning entails activities such as constructing a work breakdown structure and a schedule for start and completion of the project.

▪ *Organize*   To orchestrate the resources cost-effectively so as to execute the plan. Organizing involves activities such as forming a team, allocating resources, calculating costs, assessing risk, preparing project documentation, and ensuring good communications.

▪ *Control*   To assess how well a project meets its goals and objectives. Controlling involves collecting and assessing status reports, managing changes to baselines, and responding to circumstances that can negatively impact the project participants.

▪ *Close*   To conclude a project efficiently and effectively. Closing a project involves compiling statistics, releasing people, and preparing the lessons learned document.

CLASSICAL VS. BEHAVIORAL APPROACHES TO MANAGING PROJECTS

The field of project management is currently in transition. What worked in the past may not necessarily work in the future, precisely because the world of business has changed. In the past, managing a project meant focusing on three key elements of a project: cost, schedule, and quality. Each element had a direct relationship with the other two. Do something to one and the other two would be affected, positively or negatively. This viewpoint is considered the classical approach for managing projects. The classical approach emphasized the formal, structural aspects. Managing projects meant building neat organizational charts and highly logical schedules, as well as using formal decision-making disciplines.

Recently, however, project management has taken a more behavioral approach. The emphasis is shifting toward viewing a project as a total system, or subsystem operating within a system. This system perspective emphasizes the human aspects of a project as much as the structural ones. This does not mean that the formal tools, techniques, and principles are less important; it is just that they share the stage with behavioral techniques. The three elements—cost, schedule, and quality—gain an added dimension: people. Cost, schedule, quality, and people all play integral roles in the success or failure of a project.

Indeed, it is quite evident that the behavioral aspects of a project can have an impact on final results. Individual and team motivations, informal power structures, and interpersonal communications can have as much an effect as a poorly defined schedule or an ill-defined goal. In many cases, the impact of behavioral problems can be even more dramatic.

THE PROJECT CYCLE AND ITS PHASES

In the classical approach, project management was conceived in a linear way, or was at least formally portrayed that way. Project managers were to define, plan, organize, control, and close—in that order. While it made sense, the reality was usually something else.

Today, we view the project manager's role differently; although project managers perform the same functions, we perceive their performance not in a linear context but in a cyclical one, as shown in Exhibit 1-1. Each time the cycle completes (reaches closure), it begins again, requiring the reinstitution or refinement of the functions that were used in a previous cycle.

Exhibit 1-1. Functions of project management.

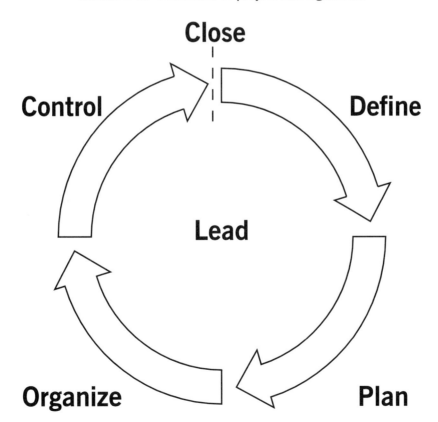

Notice the word *lead* in the middle of the cycle. As noted earlier, this function occurs throughout the project life cycle and plays a prominent role in each iteration of the cycle. It is the center—focus—to ensure that each function occurs efficiently and effectively.

The typical project cycle consists of phases that result in output. During the *concept phase,* the idea of a project arises and preliminary cost and schedule estimates are developed at a high level to determine if the project not only is technically feasible but also will have a payback. In the *formulation phase,* the complete project plans are developed. These plans often include a statement of work, a work breakdown structure, and schedules.

The *implementation phase* is when the plan is executed. Energy is expended to achieve the goals and objectives of the project in the manner prescribed during the formulation phase. Then, in the *installation phase,* the final product is delivered to the customer. At this point, considerable training and administrative support are provided to "please the customer."

The *sustaining phase* covers the time the product, such as a computing system or a building, is under the customer's control and an infrastructure exists to maintain and enhance the product. Sometimes these phases occur linearly; other times, they overlap. Still other times they occur in a spiral, as shown in Exhibit 1-2.

In today's fast-paced environment, partly owing to time-to-market pressures and partly to a rapidly changing business environment, there's pressure to accelerate the project cycle without sacrificing quality. Many projects are on the fast track, meaning they proceed quickly. To accommodate that acceleration, companies adopt simplistic, modular approaches

Exhibit 1-2. Phases of project management.

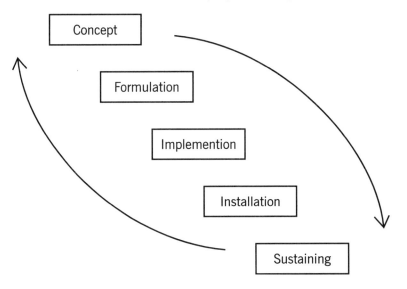

to building a new product or delivering a new service. Component-based manufacturing, reuse, and just-in-time delivery, as well as more sophisticated tools (e.g., in-systems development) for building products, enable such fast-tracking to become possible and prevalent.

PROJECT SUCCESS OR FAILURE

Projects, of course, are not operated in a vacuum. They are parts, or subsystems, of much bigger systems called businesses. Each project has or uses elements such as processes, participants, policies, procedures, and requirements, some of which are dependent upon and interact with related elements in the larger business system. A conflict between project and system can result in disequilibrium. But by taking a systems perspective, the project manager can see how all the elements interact, and assess the impact on the individual project. For example, it becomes easier to understand the impact of a 10 percent budget cut on each element of a project. More important, it is easier to identify potential project failure by recognizing the disequilibrium. If left unmanaged, disequilibrium can result in project failure.

So what types of disequilibrium make a project a success or failure? In the past, the view was that failure resulted from not adequately defining, planning, organizing, or controlling the project in a step-by-step manner. In many cases, a project's failure was attributed to not having an adequate statement of work, a work breakdown structure, or a schedule. But, as mentioned earlier, failure of a project is increasingly seen as a result of bad behavioral circumstances—for example, poor customer commitment, lack of vision, low morale, no buy-in from people doing the work, or unrealistic expectations. Such behavioral factors are frequently recognized as having as much importance for project success, for example, as a well-defined work breakdown structure. Exhibit 1-3 shows some common reasons for project success or failure.

The key, of course, is being able to recognize if and when projects start to fail. To do that requires maintaining a feedback loop throughout the project cycle. And the effectiveness of the feedback loop depends on a constant flow of quality information among the project manager, team members, the customer, and senior management; see Exhibit 1-4. We'll discuss this in greater depth in Chapters 13, 14, and 19.

Based on the case study presented in the next chapter, you will learn how to apply the basic functions of project management throughout the cycle of a typical project. Chapters 4 through 17 will walk you through the pro-

Exhibit 1-3. Reasons for project failures and successes.

Reasons for Project Failures

Classical	Behavioral
Ill-defined work breakdown structure	Inappropriate leadership style
High-level schedule	No common vision
No reporting infrastructure	Unrealistic expectations
Too pessimistic or optimistic estimates	Poor informal communications and interpersonal relationships
No change management discipline	No "buy-in" or commitment from customer or people doing work
Inadequate formal communications	Low morale
Inefficient allocation of resources	Lack of training
No accountability and responsibility for results	Poor teaming
Poor role definition	Culture not conducive to project management
Inadequacy of tools	Lack of trust among participants
Ill-defined scope	False or unrealistic expectations
Unclear requirements	No or weak executive sponsorship
Too high, too long, or too short time frame	Mediocre knowledge transfer

⌒⌒⌒

Reasons for Project Successes

Classical	Behavioral
Well-defined goals and objectives	Agreement over goals and objectives
Detailed work breakdown structure	Commitment to achieving goals and objectives
Clear reporting relationships	High morale
Formal change management disciplines in place	Good teaming
Channels of communication exist	Cooperation among all participants
Adherence to scope	Receptivity to positive and negative feedback
Reliable estimating	Receptive culture to project management
Reliable monitoring and tracking techniques	Realistic expectations
Clear requirements	Good conflict resolution
Reasonable time frame	Executive sponsorship
Broad distribution of work	Good customer-supplier relationship

Exhibit 1-4. Feedback loop.

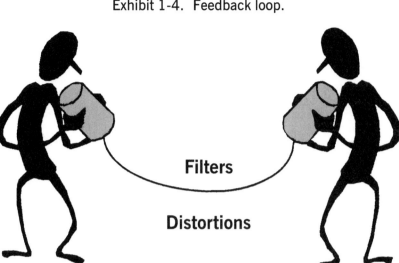

cess, showing the major assessments and decisions to be made. At the end of each chapter is a set of questions you can answer on your own to help you apply the principles and techniques that you have learned. So begin now, by meeting the CEO of Great Weddings, Inc., and the project the company is about to launch.

Chapter 2

A Wedding in Naples: Background Information on Our Case Study

Here is the case study that forms the backbone of this handbook. It is a model situation around which we have built our guidelines for effective and successful project management, using the functions of leading, defining, planning, organizing, controlling, and closing.

Great Weddings, Inc. (GWI), located in New York City, provides a full line of wedding services: sending announcements to friends, relatives, and newspapers; providing prewedding parties and rehearsals (e.g., bachelor parties and bridal showers); determining the ceremony and reception locations; arranging for travel and hotel accommodations, food and beverages; preparing and mailing invitations; providing wedding attire, flowers, sound, lighting, music, entertainment, decorations and props, photography and videotaping; coordinating wedding transportation; and preparing the wedding feast and cake.

GWI provides wedding services in fourteen states. In 1997, its revenue was $5 million after it was in business for seven years. Amelia Rainbow is president and CEO of GWI, which is privately owned, and she holds 100 percent of the stock.

Growth for the business has been slowing in recent years, from 10 percent annually three years ago to 2 percent this year. If this trend continues, the business could stagnate—or, worse, it might have to reduce services.

ORGANIZATIONAL STRUCTURE

Amelia Rainbow has several department heads at vice-presidential levels reporting to her. Each department has a corporate staff reporting to her.

All weddings are managed out of its corporate headquarters in New York City. The organizational structure of GWI is shown in Exhibit 2-1.

General Nature of the Business

GWI frequently receives solicitations for proposals. These requests are for weddings of all sizes and religions. A proposal request is a formal document sent to potential vendors. It states the requirements and expectations of the client, as well as the terms and conditions of the contract. A reply to a proposal request provides vendors with the opportunity to describe the who, what, when, where, and how for meeting the proposal's request.

A proposal has three major components: technical, management, and cost. The technical component includes:

- Vendor's experience/expertise with similar projects
- List of equipment
- Photographs of end products
- Services

Exhibit 2-1. GWI organizational chart.

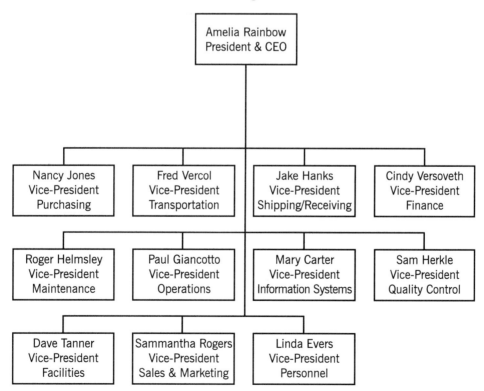

- Standards (e.g., levels of acceptance)
- Technical approach

The management component includes:

- Background
- Facilities
- Legal/contracts
- Operating plan
- Organizational structure
- Project management methodology/approach
- Program/project plan (to achieve goals and objectives)
- Résumé of cadre (key) personnel
- Resource allocation
- Schedule
- Statement of work
- Subcontract work (e.g., names of subcontractors and experience/ expertise)

The cost component includes:

- Cost for subcontract work (e.g., labor rates, equipment rental)
- Options
- Payment schedule
- Price breakout (for services and products)
- Taxes
- Type of contract (e.g., lump sum, fixed price)
- Warranties

There are three types of proposal requests: letter request, request for information, and request for proposal. The major difference among them is the level of effort and resources needed for a response and commitment upon notification of winning the contract. A *letter request* briefly conveys the needs of the client. A *request for information* usually seeks clarification about specific areas of technology. It does not require the vendor to provide any services or render any commitments. It often precedes an opportunity to respond to a request for proposal. And a *request for proposal* is a detailed, complex contract opportunity. High costs and levels of effort are necessary to prepare and respond to it.

AN OPPORTUNITY ARISES

One day, GWI receives a request to host a large wedding from the Smythes, a wealthy American family. The Smythes recently returned from a two-week trip to Naples, Italy, where they fell in love with the city. Their oldest daughter, Karen, also recently accepted a marriage proposal from her long-time boyfriend, John Hankle, who accompanied the family on their Naples trip. Everyone has agreed to hold the wedding in Naples.

Amelia recognizes that the wedding could provide the opportunity to open up a niche that GWI had until now not tapped—American wedding firms providing services in other countries. Such a wedding would be unprecedented, both in location and in size. Amelia knows, however, that it will enable GWI to avoid stagnation and grow in a highly competitive industry.

Amelia realizes that she has no choice but to use the existing infrastructure to handle such an unprecedented project. The entire wedding will also be competing with other ongoing wedding activities. Such weddings, too, are considered unprecedented opportunities, meaning that hiring more staff now might mean later laying off people or absorbing costs that could hurt GWI in the future. Amelia also recognizes that this wedding must be treated more carefully than most because of its high visibility and the amount of money being spent.

The wedding, she knows, is an excellent candidate for applying solid project management disciplines. The wedding itself has all the criteria for being a project. It has a defined product, which is a wedding. It has definite start and stop dates. It has a sequence of activities that are required to make the wedding a reality. Finally, it is temporary. Once the wedding is over—unless, of course, the idea catches on—people and other resources will be returned to "normal" business life.

THE INITIAL PROCESS

Prior to responding to the wedding request, Amelia forms a proposal team to develop the response. She appoints a proposal manager, Dave Renberg. Dave forms a team of wedding experts and a technical writer.

Dave and his team verify that the wedding will support the strategic plan. Then they conduct an internal assessment to determine whether GWI has the capabilities to support the project and it does. Next, they perform an assessment to determine the risks that GWI might face if it takes on the project and what measures to employ to prevent or mitigate those risks. GWI finds it has the capabilities to respond to the risks, although they stretch the company to the limits.

The team is then ready for the next step: prepare the proposal. After the team completes the first draft, Dave establishes an internal review team to critique the proposal. The internal review team consists of people with finance, legal, and wedding backgrounds. After several iterations, the proposal is available for Amelia's signature. After carefully reviewing its con-

---

What Type of Project Manager Are *You?*

In *Corporate Pathfinders* (New York: Penguin Books, 1987), Harold J. Leavitt identifies three types of managers in an organizational setting: problem solvers, implementers, and pathfinders.

1. The manager who is a *problem solver* emphasizes the use of reasoning, logic, and analysis. A key characteristic is reliance on facts and data.
2. The manager who is an *implementer* emphasizes the use of action through people. A key characteristic is reliance on human emotions and persuasion.
3. The manager who is a *pathfinder* emphasizes the use of visioning. A key characteristic is the importance placed on values and beliefs.

If a project requires vision, then choose a pathfinder as leader. If a project requires trouble fixing or hard logical analysis (e.g., defining requirements and specifications), then a problem solver would make the best choice. If a project requires a person with good people skills, then an implementer would be the best choice.

---

tents, Amelia signs the proposal. Within a week, she receives notification that GWI has won the contract with the Smythe family.

The next issue for Amelia to address is to determine at what hierarchical level within the company the project should be placed and what its most appropriate structure is. One criterion is to give the project as much visibility as possible. She wants to communicate its priority. With other wedding projects occurring simultaneously, it is easy to forget this priority.

She decides to establish a steering committee to oversee the overall performance of the project. This steering committee will consist of all the vice-presidents, or their representatives, with Sam Herkle of Quality as chair. The purposes of the steering committee are to provide general oversight of and guidance to the project. The steering committee will have a dotted-line relationship to Amelia, as shown in Exhibit 2-2.

Amelia next decides to adopt a *matrix structure* for the project itself. Although the project manager would be at the vice-presidential level, the resources must be borrowed from other organizations until the demand for this type of wedding increases in number, value, and longevity. The matrix structure enables her to tape the expertise of functional groups and

Exhibit 2-2. Organizational placement of Smythe Project.

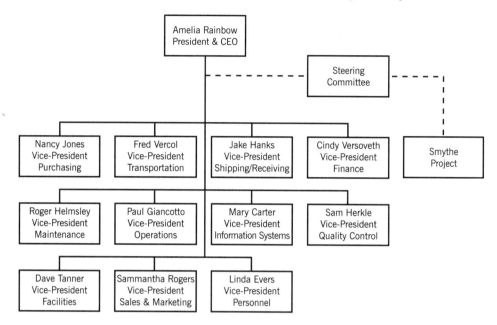

use people on a temporary basis. While completing the Smythe Project, they could also support other wedding projects.

Amelia does, however, consider a *task force structure* for the project. This structure involves assigning people as dedicated members to a project—meaning they support no other project. That would require removing people from other important projects and hiring replacements, which in turn means layoffs later on. She realizes, though, that a task force structure would grant the project more visibility and autonomy. The shortage of skills, the need for supporting existing weddings, and the temporary and risky nature of the project make the matrix structure the most appropriate selection. See Exhibit 2-3 for a comparison of these structure types.

SELECTION OF THE PROJECT MANAGER

The final initial step is to select the right person to serve as project manager. Amelia recognizes the importance of selecting the right person—his or her qualities have a direct impact on the outcome of the wedding. That's why she looks first and foremost at the leadership qualities of the person. After all, many qualified people can do the mechanics of project management, but not everyone is a project leader.

After making a few mistakes in the past, Amelia has learned that the technically competent person is not necessarily a competent project leader. A person may have the best logical and analytical mind in the group

Exhibit 2-3. Task vs. matrix structure.

Task Structure	Matrix Structure
Advantages ▪ Autonomous ▪ Dedicated resources ▪ Greater control over people ▪ Greater decision-making authority ▪ High visibility	Advantages ▪ Access to expertise not ordinarily available ▪ Flexibility in adopting to changing circumstances ▪ Less idle time for team members ▪ Fewer morale problems as project concludes
Disadvantages ▪ Impacted by turnover ▪ Less flexibility to adapt to changing circumstances ▪ Threat to morale as project winds down	Disadvantages ▪ Conflict with other projects of higher priority ▪ High stress due to conflicting demands ▪ Less autonomy ▪ Less control over people ▪ Less decision-making authority

and yet lack the qualities that lead a project to a successful conclusion. Because the project manager must interact with many people (such as sponsors, senior management, client, and team members), it is important that that person have good "people skills." These skills include:

- Active listening
- Business orientation
- Coaching
- Communication
- Conflict resolution
- Cross-functional thinking
- Customer orientation
- Delegation
- Diversity orientation
- Facilitation
- Interviewing
- Mediation
- Meetings management
- Negotiation
- Networking
- Political savvy
- Power of persuasion
- Priority setting
- Sensitivity

- Successful delivery of product
- Team building
- Time management

Of course, she also recognizes the need for additional skills:

- Communications (writing and public speaking)
- Computer literacy
- Knowledge of human resource management, procurement, and quality
- Legal affairs
- Organizational
- Planning
- Product/technical knowledge
- Risk management
- Statistics and mathematics

Finally, Amelia recognizes that the project manager must have certain personality characteristics:

- Analytical
- Can deal with uncertainty and ambiguity
- Conceptual
- Creative
- Delivers a product or service
- Exhibits courage
- Facilitates
- Flexible and adaptable
- Has high ethical standards
- Has self-confidence
- Has self-control
- Innovative
- Looks at the overall picture
- Maintains accountability
- Maintains credibility
- Makes decisions
- Mediates
- Remains open-minded
- Self-reliant and independent
- Solves problems
- Stays focused
- Takes risks
- Trustworthy
- Understands legal matters
- Willing to change and provide recognition

The Power of the Project Manager

Power is often defined as the ability to influence key players in the decision-making process to achieve a goal. In other words, power means getting what one wants.

Project managers often feel powerless because they lack the powers of functional managers, such as hiring and firing. While true, they are not as powerless as they think. According to management theorists John French and Bertram Raven, five different sources of power exist. Each applies to varying extents to the project manager.

- *Coercive power* uses fear as a primary tool. It involves inflicting punishment. Project managers usually have little coercive power in an overt sense. On a more subtle level, however, they may not assign certain people to coveted tasks, not invite them to meetings, or not communicate with them.

- *Reward power* uses positive financial and nonmonetary tools. Most project managers lack the power to use monetary incentives. However, they can provide feedback to functional managers on performance, which in turn provides a basis for determining salary increases. Project managers can also pay for training and dispense other perks. From a nonmonetary perspective, they can reward people by assigning them to high-visibility tasks, as well as involve them in the decision-making process.

- *Legitimate power* is the authority granted by the institution. In other words, such power allows managers to "order" people with the full backing of the institution. Project managers, especially in a matrix environment, lack this power—they must use other power sources. Still, they have some legitimate power, especially if they have the political support of a powerful senior manager.

- *Expert power* is based on a person's knowledge credentials, expertise, or education. Project managers are often chosen for these characteristics and they gain considerable power in this regard. The only problem is that project managers often become narrowly focused, failing to see the big picture and working on other key areas. In addition, they have power only as long as people respect those characteristics.

- *Referent power* is based on trait theory—that is, a person's characteristics. These project managers have certain characteristics that make people want to follow them. An example of such a trait is charisma.

In the end, she wants someone who can lead groups of people as well as individuals, provide a vision of what the project is to achieve, be able to communicate effectively, ensure that people stay focused on the vision, motivate people to participate, and facilitate and expedite performance. After conversations with executives on the steering committee and after reviewing the performance records of prospective candidates, Amelia selects Perry Fitzberg as the project manager.

At this point, you have seen the initial steps taken by senior management in assessing the worth of the project, evaluating its prospects for success, and establishing the responsibility for project management. Review the following questions, then move on to Chapter 3, where the qualities of project leadership are considered from a broad perspective.

Questions for Getting Started

1. What type of organizational structure does your project have? Is it task force? Matrix?
2. What soft skills will you need to lead your project? Do you know what areas to improve upon?
3. What hard skills will you need to lead your project? Do you know what areas to improve upon?
4. What aspects of your personality will prove useful in leading your project? Do you know what aspects to improve upon?
5. How will you provide a vision of what the project is to achieve?
6. Do you communicate effectively?
7. How will you ensure that people stay focused on the vision?
8. Do you have ideas for motivating people to participate?
9. Can you facilitate and expedite their performance?
10. What ideas do you have for leading groups of people?

Chapter 3

The Qualities of Good Leadership

Our concept of leadership has evolved over the years. The term was once confused with management, but today the two are distinct roles, each with its own characteristics. Rather than debate a definition of *leadership,* it is advantageous to discuss what leaders do. That way, you can come around to a better, fuller understanding of the concept.

WHAT LEADERS DO

It is increasingly clear that leaders do more than plan, organize, control, coordinate, and budget. While such activities are important and must be done, project leadership goes beyond those functions. In other words, leadership involves more than being logical, analytical, and sequential— that is, it's more than simply applying the mental thought processes originating in the left side of the brain.

Leadership takes on a holistic perspective by including the "people side" in project management, and it embraces the future rather than preserves the status quo. Thus, leadership is dynamic rather than static. It involves looking at the present and determining the steps to move on to some desired future state (e.g., a vision buttressed with meaningful goals that serve as guideposts). Leadership, not surprisingly, requires being results-oriented. By developing a vision and goals, the project leader gives the team a sense of purpose. The leader also helps align people and other resources to focus on achieving results, thereby increasing project efficiency and effectiveness. Consequently, the emphasis is on what and why rather than how. At all times, judgments are based on the big picture, which is the vision.

Leadership embraces change. It requires constantly asking, "What are we doing? Is that the only way to do it? Can we do it better?" Questioning the status quo is characteristic of leadership. It requires viewing a constantly changing environment while pursuing the vision. This emphasis on change therefore requires a willingness to adopt new processes, procedures, and roles if they will more efficiently and effectively help attain the vision. Flexibility and adaptability are two characteristics of good leadership.

Leadership means the ability to motivate. Contemporary leadership theories and practices emphasize the people side. Leadership entails active listening techniques in conflict management, "reading" people to understand their messages and motives, negotiating through open communication, and "thinking outside the box," all in an effort to attain the vision.

From a motivational perspective, leadership is getting people to perform enthusiastically, confidently, and in a highly committed way. It implies delegating, empowering, coaching, building trust, handling diversity (people from different cultures and disciplines), laying the groundwork for creativity, and facilitating performance. Leadership involves communicating. Communication is not just giving effective presentations; it is also listening to the "want to hears" and the "need to hears." It requires communicating laterally and vertically in a manner that is open and engenders trust. It means being open and honest at all times—that is, creating an atmosphere of trust, where hidden agendas and dishonesty have no place. All decisions and behaviors are of the highest ethical standards, to ensure credibility and trustworthiness up, down, and across the chain of command.

Leadership requires a constancy of purpose. It means keeping the vision in the forefront of everyone's mind by continually asking the question, "How will this help to achieve the vision?" That translates to being results-oriented and aligning responses and processes in a focused, disciplined manner.

Here, too, leadership involves a willingness to take smart, calculated risks. Leaders look for better ways not only to conduct business but also to take action. They embrace ambiguity and complexity in a manner that fosters innovative ideas and solutions to achieve the vision. They build cohesive teams that have synergy. Team members share information and other resources in a way that encourages cross-functional participation. Leaders build an atmosphere of trust and mutual support, emphasizing relational rather than hierarchical interactions and directing team energy toward achieving the vision. Thus, leadership means facilitating rather than impeding performance. Leaders help people do their jobs in a positive, not negative, way. They remove obstacles to performance, not create them. They secure the resources. However, they do more. They can maneuver through the "halls of power," network with key players, and interact with the customer to ensure satisfaction of all requirements and specifications. In addition, they can be political if it furthers the interests of the project.

Finally, leaders put the customer first. They strive to understand everything about the customer—for example, needs, tastes, and relevant market conditions. The customer is king and drives the vision; without that focus on the vision, the project becomes quixotic.

WHEN LEADERSHIP FALTERS OR IS MISSING

Leadership encourages greater productivity. An experienced team member or project manager only has to work once on a project to understand the difference between a project with leadership and one without it. But being a project manager has never been harder. The days of managing the team with "thou shalts," with the support of a clearly designed organizational structure and rational, logical discipline, are over. Good project managers know the value of exercising effective leadership throughout the project cycle. They know that the leader must inspire the team to accomplish goals and objectives at a level that meets, even exceeds, expectations.

That is not as simple as it sounds. The people to be inspired are not just the ones working directly on the project. They are also the ones whom the leader reports to (e.g., customer and senior management) and those who support the project for a short period of time (e.g., contract employees and consultants). With all these players, in a constantly changing environment, effective leadership is critical.

Although leadership is important for a project, it rarely is seen on some projects. The reasons for this are many, and are worth noting.

1. There is a tendency to select people solely for their technical expertise. While expertise is important, it is a mistake to assume that expertise is equivalent to leadership. Leadership goes beyond technical prowess, increasingly recognized as subordinate to other qualities. Often, a person selected for his or her technical expertise relies on that quality at the expense of the project.

2. There is a failure to distinguish between project leadership and project management. Project management deals with the mechanics of managing a project, such as building a schedule; project leadership deals with much bigger issues—for example, ensuring that people focus on the vision. (See box on page 25.)

3. There is a tendency to wear blinders. In a complex, constantly changing environment, many project managers seek security by grabbing on to a small piece rather than looking at the big picture. They may focus, for example, solely on technical issues or on the schedule at the expense of more important areas.

4. There is a tendency to be heroic. That is, they try to do everything themselves and be all things to all people. They eventually start to overcon-

---

Project Management vs. Project Leadership

Is there a difference between project management and project leadership?

Project management uses the tools, knowledge, and techniques needed for defining, planning, organizing, controlling, leading, and closing a project. Project leadership appears, therefore, to be a subset of project management. But it would be a mistake to assume that project leadership is secondary to project management. Project leadership is the only function that occurs throughout the project cycle. It is, in many ways, the glue that holds the other functions together. The output from defining, planning, organizing, controlling, and closing a project depends largely on how well project leadership is exhibited. Without solid leadership, performance of the other functions will be marginal at best.

Industries are replete with examples of projects that had well-defined plans and plenty of financial support, yet achieved less than satisfactory results. Project managers must gain and retain the confidence of myriad players, including the project sponsor, client, team, and senior management. Project leadership, then, means going beyond the mechanics of managing a project, such as building a work breakdown structure, constructing schedules, or managing change. It calls for inspiring all players to accomplish the goals and objectives in a manner that meets or exceeds expectations.

---

trol and in the end, as many experienced project managers know, control very little, even themselves. They fail, for example, to delegate.

5. There is a tendency to emphasize hard rather than soft skills. Hard skills are scheduling and statistical analysis; soft skills are active listening and writing. It is not uncommon for project managers of technical projects to disparagingly refer to soft skills as "touchy-feely." Yet time and again, studies have shown that soft skills can prove as critical, indeed more so, in a project's success.

6. There is a tendency to select project managers based on the FBI (*F*riends, *B*rothers, and *In*-laws) principle. Senior managers often select people they like or who are like themselves, who may or may not have the attributes of a project leader.

7. There is a tendency by senior management to micromanage a project. They treat the project as a pet, smothering it with attention, thereby

killing any initiative by the project manager or the team. An example is requiring any action, even the smallest, to have approval from senior management. Such an oppressive atmosphere makes it impossible to exercise project leadership.

8. There is a failure to recognize that leadership is ongoing. It starts at the beginning and continues throughout the project cycle. Yet especially with long-term projects, managers tend to forget about inspiring people and their leadership assumes a posture of benign neglect.

9. There is a tendency to ignore or not recognize the indicators of poor leadership. These indicators include a high turnover or absenteeism rate among team members, repetitive problems with the quality of output, and constant slippage of major milestone dates. Of course, these indicators may reflect other problems; however, there's a high correlation between problems in leadership and those in performance.

10. There is a tendency toward window dressing rather than dealing with substantive issues. Window dressing concentrates on images; substantive issues probe the root causes. While looking good has its immediate advantages, too much emphasis on image can have deleterious effects as the underlying problems persist and become more acute.

ARE LEADERS BORN OR MADE?

For a long time, people have debated whether leaders were born or made. The issue remains relatively unsettled, although most management experts believe that leaders are made rather than born. Basically, there are three theories of leadership: trait theories, situational contingency theories, and personal behavior theories.

1. *Trait theorists* say that people contain characteristics that make them leaders. These characteristics could be based on personality, internal motivations, physical features, or a combination of two or more.
2. *Situational contingency theorists* deal with different leadership styles under varying circumstances. Typical leadership styles are either task or people centered and, depending on the circumstances, one style is preferable to another.
3. *Personal behavior theorists* deal with views on how leaders perceive people and their role in an organization. Some managers stress the people side while others emphasize the mission.

Regardless of approach, the contemporary viewpoint is that managers in general and project managers in particular stress people rather than task completion. So if you are currently a project manager—or strive to become one—keep the leadership qualities discussed in this chapter foremost in your mind.

It is our hope, of course, that you will avoid these pitfalls and become an effective, successful project leader. Part II begins with the initial steps of project management and concludes with a chapter on closure. The latter discusses how to learn from past mistakes so that future projects will have successful outcomes.

Part II

The Basic Functions of Project Management

Chapter 4

The Vision Statement and Motivating for Project Success

Perry Fitzberg, newly appointed manager for GWI's Smythe Project, knows all too well that leadership involves more than just building schedules and calculating budgets. As project manager it will be his job to:

1. Provide a vision of what the project is to achieve.
2. Communicate that vision to all involved.
3. Ensure that everyone stays focused on that vision.
4. Motivate people to participate in the project.
5. Facilitate and expedite performance.
6. Build an effective team.

But let's examine each of these points, one at a time.

PROVIDING THE PROJECT VISION

From a project management perspective, the *vision* describes what the project is to achieve. It is often a high-level statement supported by a list of goals and objectives. The vision is essentially an idea of some desired end state, expressed in a form that everyone understands, can relate to, and can feel a sense of commitment to.

Perry knows that the vision should be clear, concise, and direct. He used several sources to draft the statement, including the minutes of meetings and the formal contract with the customer. Perry also knows that the vision statement will require commitment by people working directly and indirectly on the project. To engender this commitment, he solicits feedback to make revisions where appropriate. This helps generate commitment, encourages raising important questions, and possibly addresses communciation problems before they can negatively impact the project. Exhibit 4-1 is his vision statement for the Smythe Project.

Having a vision statement at the outset offers several advantages:

1. It clearly formulates in people's minds what the project is to achieve. In other words, it communicates the scope of the project, helping to avoid "scope creep," that is, unintentional expansion of the project's boundaries.

2. It provides a basis for managing the project. All subsequent activities are planned, organized, and controlled from the perspective of that vision. "Mapping" becomes easier because everyone knows what perspective to take.

3. It bridges the communications gap. Since a vision statement describes what the project is to achieve, there's less chance for ambiguity as people understand the importance of their activities.

4. The vision statement provides a basis for evaluating performance. Throughout the project cycle, questions will arise about performance. The vision statement is the yardstick against which performance can be judged.

5. It determines the importance of questions that arise during the project. What is important and what is not must always be clear. A vision statement is the tool to help answer those questions.

6. The vision statement empowers, it gives people a means for independent judgment. Essentially it is the criterion for decision making.

COMMUNICATING THE VISION

A vision statement is worthless, of course, unless other people know about it. Therefore, Perry widely distributes the statement. He ensures that the right people receive the statement at the right time.

Making the vision statement public has obvious benefits, which are important to state here. For example, it gives people a sense of the scope of the project. It establishes the groundwork for effective communication

Exhibit 4-1. Vision statement.

Smythe Project Vision Statement
Provide a wedding with the grandest of flair, which all attendees will talk about for years to come and which will bring joy and happiness to the families of the newlyweds.

via a common language and mental framework. Finally, it helps build a sense of community.

But the challenges of communication are many. Mental paradigms, values, beliefs, and attitudes, for example, may restrict how the vision statement is received. People tend to filter or slant the message. Also, "pockets of resistance" exist, reflecting nonacceptance of the vision. That resistance might be covert (subtle, negative comments) or overt (vocalizing opposition). Another challenge is to cut through the layers of bureaucracy. Organizational layers may filter or alter the message, either intentionally or inadvertently.

So Perry will publish the vision statement in a house newsletter. He will post it on the project's Web site. He will conduct information-sharing sessions or give presentations. He'll provide a copy for each project manual and reiterate it at training sessions and other meetings. (Chapters 13, 14, and 19 have additional information on communciation.) The key is to ensure the vision statement is brought to everyone's attention.

KEEPING PEOPLE FOCUSED ON THE VISION

Perry realizes that it is easy to get sidetracked—that is, to lose sight of the vision while "fighting fires." He is concerned about not letting those fires distract him or the team. If they become distracted the likelihood increases for the schedule to slide, the project to overrun the budget, and the output to be inferior.

As project manager, Perry takes the lead in asking whether each process, activity, or action will achieve the vision. He continually raises the issue of direction, although he wants everyone to do the same. And there are several ways he can ensure that people stay focused, such as collecting and evaluating data regarding schedule and budget; tracking past performance and projecting the future; identifying likely risks and ways to respond; instituting change management disciplines; and collecting and evaluating measurements and metrics on quality. Chapters 15 and 16 will describe methods for data collection. Of course, Perry does not do this alone. He obtains help from team players to validate his assessments.

FACILITATING AND EXPEDITING PERFORMANCE

Most project teams do not operate in a vacuum. They face obstacles and frustrations, such as not having the right equipment or having to deal with bureaucratic politics. In addition, project managers can frustrate or facilitate the performance of team members.

Perry, of course, wants to facilitate rather than impede performance.

He faces constraints on his power, yet he refuses to take a "dying cockroach" position. He strives to eliminate physical distractions (e.g., noisy equipment), to ensure the availability of the right tools (e.g., telecommunication equipment and software), to shield the team from administrative red tape (e.g., computing paperwork), and to handle the political aspects of the project (e.g., interference in daily activities by senior management).

Perry does not address every problem or obstacle that confronts the team. But he determines what is important, in light of whether it affects the achievement of the vision.

MOTIVATION TO PARTICIPATE

Perry understands that, without people, the project does not exist. He also knows that without *motivated* people, performance will suffer. To motivate his team, Perry must have insight into human behavior and direct it toward achieving the vision.

Motivation deals with the internal conditions that encourage people to act or not to act. It is a complex process that remains intriguing to psychologists and layman alike. From Sigmund Freud and Carl Jung to contemporary practitioners, the mystery of human behavior remains, despite growth in our knowledge. From a managerial perspective, there are many theories that work most of the time, but not always, and have proved useful for project managers like Perry.

Credit for the birth of motivational theory largely falls to Frederick Taylor, a major contributor to the development of the concept of *scientific management.* He relied on identifying the most efficient tasks to perform a job, training people to do them, developing standards to measure performance, and separating tasks between management and workers. The best workers—the ones meeting or exceeding the standard—received the best pay.

Over the years, it has become quite clear that scientific management, albeit revolutionary, had negative motivational consequences. Work often became meaningless and highly routine, and management relied solely on financial motivations. But since Taylor, other motivational theroies have been developed.

One is Frederick Herzberg's two-factor theory of motivation. According to this, people are motivated via maintenance (hygiene) or motivational factors (motivators). *Maintenance factors* are dissatisfiers, meaning that if not present to a sufficient degree, they will negatively impact motivation. Maintenance factors include pay, policies, and work conditions. *Motivational factors* are satisfiers, meaning that if addressed, they will positively impact performance. Motivational factors include opportunities for achievement, recognition, and advancement.

Abraham Maslow's *hierarchy of needs* is another popular motivational theory. According to this, people are motivated by five fundamental needs, in the following order: physiological, safety, love/belongingness, self-esteem, and self-actualization. Each need must be satisfied sequentially.

Physiological needs are ones like food, sex, and water. Safety needs include psychological and physical security. Love/belongingness needs include social acceptability. Self-esteem needs include feeling good and confident about oneself. Self-actualization needs include realizing one's full potential.

Other motivational theories are more narrowly focused. According to David C. McClelland's *n Ach theory,* people have a need to achieve; the degree just varies from person to person. He found that this need was influenced by the expectation of success and the likelihood of reward. If a manager combines the two, there's a greater the probability of achieving successful results. Victor Vroom developed another theory of motivation based on an individual's goal and the influence different behaviors have in achieving that goal. If people feel a goal is important, they will select the appropriate behavior that promises the highest probability of success. Hence, motivation depends on whether people place much value on a goal.

Motivational theories have laid the foundation for managerial theories. One of those is Douglas McGregor's *Theory X* and *Theory Y.* The Theory X style of management involves taking a negative view of human nature. Managers believe people dislike work, will avoid it, accept little or no responsibility, and consequently need close oversight, maybe even coercion. But Theory Y takes a positive view of human nature. Managers believe people like work and, if the rewards and conditions are right, will commit themselves to their jobs and take on responsibility—consequently, close oversight is unnecessary.

Research known as the Michigan studies has revealed two types of supervisory styles that can affect motivation: production and employee-centered. Production-centered supervisors are task-oriented. They treat people as instruments of production and intervene on how to perform the work; they tend to be autocratic in their style. Employee-centered supervisors are people-oriented. They grant autonomy to people when performing tasks, take a positive view of the capabilities and talents of subordinates, and tend to be democratic in their style. The studies found that employee-centered supervisors generally achieve the best performance.

Perry recognizes that the trend in managing people is increasingly to emphasize the people side. A dramatic shift has occurred away from being task or mission oriented and toward taking a behaviorist approach. Project managers, especially, must be sensitive to this shift because they often lack command and control. They must rely on positive motivation to have people perform tasks and must understand how their own behavior affects that of others.

Keeping the above theories in mind, Perry uses some powerful motivational tools:

Delegation

Because some project managers feel powerless (e.g., they lack command and control over people), they equate that with a loss of control and to compensate, do many tasks themselves. The results are frequently poor because they assume too much work. The work piles up and the schedule slides. The answer, as Perry knows, is to delegate.

Delegating is having one person act on behalf of another. This means relinquishing authority to perform the work but not necessarily the responsibility or accountability for the results. A reluctance to delegate often indicates lack of confidence in oneself or the delegate. It manifests itself through comments like "I can do a better job myself."

Perry is a practical person who knows that delegation can have negative consequences, too. To ensure that he delegates work correctly, he looks at the nature and importance of the tasks, the capabilities and personality of the individuals, and the availability of time and other resources.

Job rotation, Enlargement, and Enrichment

Job rotation entails moving people from one job to another to increase their overall awareness or exposure. It is useful for inculcating a generalist background and providing a "bit picture" viewpoint. *Job enlargement* involves increasing the number of tasks and responsibilities to perform. It increases the level of effort and challenge. *Job enrichment* entails structuring or assessing tasks and responsibilities to give people the opportunity to actualize.

Applying all three tools requires careful consideration. Perry must ponder the personality, talents, expertise, and knowledge of each individual. He must also consider nonbehavioral factors such as the availability of time, importance of the task, learning curve, cost, and impact to quality.

Participation

Commitment is important to a project's success. If lacking, then people will not care about the results. Perry knows a powerful way to build commitment is through participation.

Participation means obtaining input or feedback prior to making a decision. Perry accomplishes that by getting feedback on the statement of work, estimates, and schedules, and getting participation at meetings. Participation breeds emotional commitment to the outcome.

Personal Goal Attainment

People have different goals—money, power, or physical surroundings—but Perry must identify the reason each person is working on the Smythe Project. This knowledge will help him satisfy a person's expectations while simultaneously achieving the overall goals of the project.

What Perry hopes to achieve is to maximize output by matching effort, performance, and project goals. To do that, Perry must know the people on the project, by holding one-on-one sessions, reviewing of personnel documentation (résumés), and personal familiarization. Only then can he motivate by satisfying the WIIFM (What's In It For Me) syndrome.

Personality/Task Match

Personality is the composite of characteristics that constitute a person's behavior. How people interact with their environment reflects their personality. One type of interaction is through the performance of tasks. Perry knows that some people are a mismatch for certain tasks. Some may not be gregarious enough to perform tasks involving social interaction; others lack the personality to deal with routine, repetitive tasks that involve methodical detail.

A mismatch between personality and task can negatively impact project performance. Tasks can go uncompleted, morale and esprit de corps can plummet, quality can suffer, and schedule can slide. To avoid such results, Perry considers several variables when matching a person to a task. From a personality perspective, he looks at the track record, including what they did and did not do well in the past; their characteristics (introversion, extroversion); intelligence; self-confidence; stress handling abilities; and needs. From a structural perspective, he also considers the complexity of the task, as well as its variety, autonomy, and scope.

Recognition

Many people want to stand out. Receiving recognition is one way to satisfy that need.

Recognition must be done carefully; otherwise, it can be counterproductive. The idea is to find a balance between individual and team recognition and to discover the types of recognition people value. Perry also knows that recognition must follow some basic principles. It must be genuine, timely, fair, objective, meaningful, and not overdone.

Stretching

Sometimes Perry will assign people to tasks that present a challenge. People view the task as more difficult than the "typical" task, but not impossible to complete. The new challenge may exceed physical and emotional dimensions, or present a mental challenge relating to intelligence, training, or aptitude. The idea is to match the person to the task so that the person "stretches" and does not "break."

One key motivational issue in recent years is the role stress plays on the project manager and the team. Perry knows that he and his team will be under considerable stress and that he has responsibility for managing it. There are two types of stress: negative stress (or distress) and positive stress (or eustress).

Negative stress manifests itself in many ways. It causes ailments, from hives to heart attacks. It affects people psychologically by making them depressed and argumentative or just "wanting to give up." It affects the performance of the team as conflict intensifies; people start "throwing their work over the fence" and they lower their productivity.

Perry is well aware that there are many causes for high stress. Downsizing, increased time-to-market pressures, rapidly varying market conditions, consultants and contractors hired as replacements, and outsourcing services all add to a stressful situation. Poor project management practices also cause stress. Such practices include not defining roles and responsibilities clearly; unrealistically assigning resources; compressing the schedules; providing inadequate tools; and not isolating the team from politics.

Perry realizes that he does not have to let stress have a harmful effect on him or his team. He can alleviate the impact in several ways. For example, he can develop and revise his project plan to reflect realism, rotate people between critical and noncritical tasks or equitably distribute the workload; provide opportunities for the team members to go on respites or breaks from time to time; assign people to tasks that are more suitable to their expertise level, intelligence type, or personality type; and encourage people to be flexible. As for Perry himself, he considers all the same for himself.

TEAM BUILDING

A team is more than just a group of people doing work. It is an assembly of individuals with diverse backgrounds who interact for a specific purpose. The idea is to capture and direct the synergy generated by the group to efficiently and effectively achieve a goal. Throughout the years, Perry has witnessed many signs of ineffective teams.

What Is Your Team-Building Style?

Decide-X, a Bellevue, Washington, company, provides a scientific tool—also called Decide-X—to measure how much information a person needs before reaching a decision.

According to Decide-X, people deal with team-building situations in ways that reflect their needs and desires, as well as their preferences in dealing with direction, change, details, and other characteristics of a work situation. There are four primary styles:

- *Reactive Stimulators* thrive on action and the immediate. They prefer situations or projects that are fast-moving and have lots of pressure.
- *Logical Processors* thrive on logical detail while maintaining focus. They prefer situations and projects with organizational structure.
- *Hypothetical Analyzers* like to solve problems using decomposition to unravel complexity. They prefer situations and projects that provide a relatively slow pace to perform analysis.
- *Relational Innovators* deal in ideas from a big-picture perspective and find relationships or patterns. They prefer situations and projects that involve blue-skying and move at a pace that allows them to do that.

From a project management perspective, the Decide-X tool is very useful. Different combinations of styles on a project team can influence the level of detail that goes into making a decision and how quickly it is done. For example, if you put a Reactive Stimulator and a Relational Innovator on a task, the questions will arise: (1) will decisions be made quickly with little attention to detail (as may be needed), or will they be made much more slowly, to allow for exploration of detail? And (2) will the Reactive Stimulator and Relational Innovator cooperate, or will they conflict?

Decide-X differs from other approaches, which focus only on the individual, because it looks at the *interactions* of people. Decide-X is described in more detail in Gary Salton, *Organizational Engineering* (Ann Arbor, Mich.: Professional Communications, 1996).

Characteristics of Poor Teams

▪ No processes for gaining consensus or resolving conflicts. Team squabbles and overt and covert discussions are ongoing occurrences, making cooperation difficult, even impossible.

▪ Team members who lack commitment to the goal. No one has an emotional attachment to the goal.

▪ No camaraderie or esprit de corps. The players do not feel that they are part of a team. Instead, everyone acts in his or her own interests.

▪ Lack of openness and trust. Everyone is guarded, protective of his or her own interests. Openness and truthfulness are perceived as yielding to someone, giving a competitive advantage, or exposing vulnerabilities.

▪ Vague role definitions. The reporting structures and responsibilities are unclear, causing conflicts. Territorial disputes and power struggles occur often.

▪ No commonality or cohesiveness. The team is an unorganized grouping of people. No one feels a sense of community or brotherhood. No common ground exists other than to meet periodically to work. This results in lost synergy.

▪ Conformity and mind protection. Insecurity permeates people for fear of being different or ostracized. People do not speak or share information unless it reinforces behavior or thoughts.

▪ Low tolerance for diversity. The pressure to conform is so intense that anyone different in thinking or work style is ostracized or not taken seriously. Whistle-blowers and creative types, for instance, may be viewed with suspicion. Under such circumstances no opportunity is available to capitalize on people's strengths and address their weaknesses.

▪ Insufficient resources. Whether it's people, equipment, supplies, facilities, time, or money, insufficient resources make teams ineffective. The situation can also lead to squabbling, dissention, even revolts. If resources are not distributed in an objective, meaningful manner, then differences can magnify into severe conflicts. Members of the team can quickly become polarized.

▪ Lack of management support. If team members perceive—whether justifiably or not—that management is not supportive of the project, then motivation can plummet. People will feel that the work is not valuable, at least to the organization.

▪ Listless team members. The goals are vague or nonexistent. Even if the goals are defined, no one—including the project manager—seems to focus on them. Instead, everyone is aimless.

▪ Discontinuity between individual expectations and group expectations. There is a misalignment between the two, with the latter not valuing the former. A symbiotic relationship between the two just does not exist.

An ineffective team is conflict ridden, filled with distrust, unfocused, and reeking of negative competition. These conditions manifest themselves in high turnover and absenteeism, considerable frustration levels, poor communication, no esprit de corps, and intolerance.

Perry wants, of course, a project team with desirable characteristics:

Characteristics of Effective Teams

- Acceptance of new ideas and objective evaluation of them
- Sustained common norms, values, and beliefs without excessive conformity
- Synergy through mutual support
- Loyalty and commitment to the project
- Focus on end results
- A trusting, open attitude
- Ability to gain consensus and resolve conflicts
- High morale and esprit de corps
- Information and resources sharing

Perry knows all too well that a team with these characteristics is difficult to achieve. Yet he also knows that such characteristics will not arise unless he takes action. There are seven actions that he takes to engender such characteristics:

1. He sets the example. He not only espouses certain values and beliefs but also exercises them. He wants people to be trustful and open, so he is trustful and open. He expects people to be committed, so he is committed. In other words, he "walks the talk."

2. He encourages communication—oral, written, and electronic. He knows that communication is more than writing memos, standing in front of a team, or setting up a Web site. It requires sharing information in an open and trusting manner, holding frequent meetings (status reviews and staff), publishing a project manual, defining acronyms and jargon, employing technology as a communications tool, and encouraging task interdependence.

3. He has the team focus on results. They direct all their energies toward achieving the vision. Whether he or the team makes a decision, it is made in the context of achieving the vision. Perry constantly communicates the vision and establishes change control and problem-solving processes.

4. He engenders high morale and esprit de corps by developing and maintaining the energy that comes from teaming. He knows, however, that he must continually nurture that energy to keep it flowing. So he empowers team members, encourages consensus building and win-win solutions,

increases task interdependence, matches the right person with the right task, and teams people with complementary work styles.

5. He builds commitment to the vision and the project. Throughout the project cycle, team commitment can rise or fall. Ideally, Perry wants to achieve the former. Ways to do that include matching people's interests with tasks, encouraging participative decision making, empowering people, seeking input and feedback, assigning people with responsibility for completing deliverables, and keeping the project in the forefront of everyone's mind.

6. He lays the groundwork for synergy. A team is more than the sum of its members. But synergy requires cooperation. Ways to obtain cooperation include providing cross-training so that people understand each other's roles and responsibilities, clearly defining roles and responsibilities, determining each team member's strengths and weaknesses and making assignments that capitalize on the former, and having groups within the team be accountable for a complete work unit (e.g., subproduct or deliverable).

7. He encourages greater diversity in thinking, work style, and behavior. Always mindful of the danger of groupthink, Perry encourages different thoughts and perspectives. He is especially aware of the multicultural environment of the Smythe Project. The project culminates in Italy and, therefore, requires working with people from another country. The Smythe family also has many friends around the world who will attend the wedding. To ensure receptivity to diversity, Perry uses cross-training and job rotation to broaden people's understanding of each other, encourages experimentation and brainstorming to develop new ideas and keep an open mind, seeks task interdependence to encourage communication, and nurtures a continuous learning environment.

TEAM DIVERSITY

With globalization of the economy in general and the Smythe Project in particular, Perry recognizes that the challenge of leading a diversified team has never been greater. The team members have a variety of backgrounds, including race, ethnicity, and religion. Leading a team in such an environment requires heightened sensitivity to different values, beliefs, norms, and lifestyles.

Perry understands that people vary in their concept of time, ways of doing business, styles of management and leadership, and views of how the world functions. He also understands that differences exist in the meaning of words (semantics), interpretation of expressions (body language), perception of priorities, and definition of team building. Needless to say, all this diversity adds complexity to the planning, coordination, and control of the project. He knows, however, that he can deal with diversity in several ways.

1. He sets the example by embracing diversity. Through research, background reviews, interviews, and the like, Perry learns about the diverse backgrounds of the people and encourages everyone to do the same.

2. He is patient when dealing with people of a different background. He remains conscious of different values and beliefs, for example, and accounts for them when leading the project.

3. He overcomes the temptation to stereotype. That is, he avoids generalizing about people based on one characteristic. He also tackles stereotyping by team members. An effective approach is to have people with different backgrounds work together. He can also have the team, with himself, attend diversity training to understand and respect differences.

4. He has empathy for other people's experiences. The word is *empathy,* not *sympathy,* since the latter connotes patronization and condescension. He attempts to appreciate, for example, the difficulties in reconciling different perceptions of time.

5. He encourages feedback. He is especially mindful to obtain feedback from people whose cultural background is dramatically different from his own or from the rest of the team. This lessens the tendency for the team to split into subgroups.

Contract Employees and Consultants

Along with downsizing has come a corresponding rise in the use of consultants and contract employees. The Smythe Project is no different, and its use of such people challenges his efforts to build a cohesive team.

Many contract employees and consultants do not feel they are part of a team. They know that their presence is temporary; their participation could end at any time; hence their commitment is questionable. At the same time, many permanent employees feel slighted by the presence of independent contractors and consultants. They feel that management is exhibiting lack of confidence in their work, or that management perceives outside help as better than inside. Team members may also feel that the contractors or consultants are receiving higher compensation or the best offices or equipment.

These circumstances, real or imagined, challenge any team-building effort. But they are not insurmountable, even for Perry. He gives preference to permanent employees regarding task assignments, equipment, and other perks. An exception is made only if the consultant or contractor has unique expertise, and, if so, preference is only for the duration of the task.

Perry also gives employees the first opportunity to participate in decision making. (More about contractors and outsourcing in Chapter 9.)

Telecommuting and Mobile Computing

In today's environment, team members may be spread over a wide geographical area, presenting little opportunity to see each other. (See Chapter 19 for additional information.) Team building can be extremely difficult, thanks to this dispersion. To foster team building, however, Perry takes three important steps:

1. He tries to have everyone on the team meet periodically. At a minimum, this meeting provides an opportunity to exchange ideas, share information, and become acquainted.

2. He develops rules of exchange or communications etiquette. For instance, colleagues should respond to each other within a certain time. Such etiquette enables greater interaction, which in turn increases bonding or cohesion.

3. He assigns people to tasks that require greater interaction and, if only occasionally, meeting physically. If meeting is costly or impossible, the task should require at least some electronic interdependence to generate cohesion.

In general, Perry treats the word TEAMING as an acronym to remind him of how to build a good project team:

*T*arget	Focus on the end result.
*E*nergize	Provide the emotional spark that encourages high morale and esprit de corps.
*A*ssemble	Bring people together with defined roles and responsibilities.
*M*ove	Get people to move efficiently and effectively toward the results.
*I*nform	Have people share knowledge, skills, and expertise, laterally and vertically.
*N*eutralize	Remove biases and preferences in decision making.
*G*lue	Keep the team as a cohesive unit so that synergy is produced.

There is additional information on telecommuting and other technology-based innovations in Chapter 19.

The Project Manager as a Motivator

Leadership plays an important role in the successful execution of a project. However, it is not something that can be done in a "paint-by-number" fashion. Perry, like all experienced project managers, knows that leadership must be constantly exercised throughout a project. It requires having a basic understanding of what motivates people.

A vision statement partly satisfies the motivational needs of a project team. Perry realizes, however, that the vision is just one aspect of leadership. He must build teams and focus all their efforts on achieving the vision. The vision plays another role too. It provides the basis for developing a meaningful statement of work.

Questions for Getting Started

1. Can you identify the obstacles for exercising effective leadership inherent in your project?
2. How will you develop a vision for your project? How do you plan to communicate it? What are the challenges you face in developing and communicating that vision? How do you plan to overcome them?
3. How will you ensure that your project stays focused on the vision? What challenges will you face?
4. How will you facilitate and expedite performance? What obstacles will you face and how will you overcome them?
5. In what ways (e.g., job enrichment) do you plan to motivate the people on your team? What challenges will you face and how do you plan to overcome them?
6. In what ways (e.g., focus on the vision) will you encourage team building? What obstacles will you face and how will you overcome them?
7. If you have contractors, consultants, or telecommuters, how will they be involved? What impact will that have on the permanent team members and what will you do about any problems that arise?

Chapter 5

The Statement of Work and the Project Announcement

Perry recognizes that a key determinant for success or failure of a project is the adequacy of the definition. As described in Chapter 1, the project manager defines the project, or determines its vision (as mentioned in Chapter 4), goals, objectives, scope, responsibilities, and deliverables. He knows that good definition lays the groundwork for developing reliable plans. It also sets the stage for effective communication throughout the project cycle.

To *define* is to determine exactly the purpose and boundaries of the project. In other words,

- What are the goals and objectives?
- Who are the principal participants?
- When must the project be finished?
- Where will the project be executed?
- How will the result be achieved?
- Why is the project being launched?
- What are the constraints/limitations of the project?

By answering such questions Perry can better execute the other functions of project management. However, getting answers to these and other questions is not easy. It requires considerable effort, largely by interviewing members of the steering committee, contacting the customer, and reviewing documentation (e.g., the contract between the company and the Smythe family).

THE STATEMENT OF WORK

Although a contract has been signed between GWI and the Smythe family, many details remain unaccounted for. Perry uses a *statement of work*

(SOW) or, more informally, a *statement of understanding* to obtain and record answers to any remaining questions.

The SOW is a definitive agreement between the customer and the project's leadership about what is to be accomplished. Perry knows, however, that the SOW is more than an agreement between the major participants. It also sets the groundwork for effective communication, raises and addresses assumptions and potential conflicts, and gives direction overall.

The SOW, then, is a medium for defining what the project will accomplish and the overall approach to take. With an SOW Perry will have the answers to five *W*'s:

1. What is the product or service to be delivered?
2. Who are the primary participants, including the customers?
3. When must the project start and be completed?
4. Where will the project be undertaken?
5. Why is there a project?

More specifically, Perry will capture the following information:

- Constraints or limitations on the work
- Coordination requirements
- Levels of support from participants
- Major assumptions
- Major responsibilities
- Milestone dates
- Quality criteria
- Specific objectives

The onus is on Perry to acquire the data necessary to draft the SOW. It is also on him to draft the document and obtain final approval. To obtain that data, Perry has several options, which include examining data from earlier, similar projects; interviewing project sponsor, steering committee, vendors, or customers; reviewing existing documentation, such as memos or procedures with earlier customers; and reviewing lessons learned, if applicable, from earlier projects.

After collecting the data, Perry prepares a draft of the SOW, which follows this outline form:

    I. Introduction
   II. Scope
  III. Assumptions
  IV. Constraints
   V. Performance Criteria
  VI. Product/Service description

The Art of Interviewing

You don't have to be a Barbara Walters or Larry King to conduct effective interviews. You just need to follow a few principles:

- Determine the objectives of the interview. Is it specific information that you need or general background information?
- Determine whether you want to do a structured or an unstructured interview.

Structured interviewing is asking a set of questions that help you get specific, often detailed information. You use it when the subject matter is clear and unambiguous. For example, use a structured interview to obtain specific information about a line item in a statement of work.

Unstructured interviewing is asking open-ended questions and winging it. The interviewer controls the interview as it progresses. You use it when the subject matter is vague and greater insight into the subject matter is necessary. For example, use an unstructured interview to obtain an understanding of the customer's expectations for a project.

Follow proper interviewing etiquette by asking permission to record or tape sessions, asking clear and concise questions, keeping emotional distance from the response, listening actively, and scheduling interview sessions at the right time. Avoid engaging in a debate and do not introduce bias in your questions.

If you follow these guidelines, interviewing will be a useful tool for acquiring information for your statement of work.

   VII. Major Responsibilities
 VIII. References
    IX. Amendments
     X. Signatures

Exhibit 5-1 shows the draft SOW that Perry has prepared. When reviewing the draft, consider the purpose of each major section.

Introduction

This section describes the goal of the project. It provides the name of the project, gives reasons for its existence, names major players, and provides other pertinent information.

The Art of Negotiation

As a project manager, you will have plenty of opportunity to negotiate. You will have to negotiate resources, schedules, budgets, and quality with customers, team members, and senior management. Sometimes the negotiation will be formal, other times it will be informal.

When negotiating, keep these principles in mind:

1. Seek a win-win solution. Negotiation is not a victory over someone. Such victories are short-lived and can cause greater problems later on.
2. Keep the commonalities between you and the person you're negotiating with in the forefront of your mind. Commonalities might include values, norms, tools, goals, or visions. By stressing what's common, you keep communication open.
3. Be flexible. A rigid stance may leave you with nothing or even a lose-lose result. Be flexible by knowing what you value most and least.
4. Pick the right time and place to negotiate, one that is comfortable for both parties. Being comfortable opens the dialogue.
5. Know as much as possible about the person you're negotiating with.

Scope

This section lists the project's "boundaries"—that is, what is and is not to be done. The scope is important for planning and also for minimizing changes.

Assumptions

This section lists any unsubstantiated ideas about the project. Assumptions may, for example, relate to levels of internal support or existing or market conditions. Assumptions are used in planning.

Constraints

Rarely does a project have unlimited resources at its disposal. Money, time, people, equipment, supplies, and facilities are often limited in quan-

Exhibit 5-1. Statement of work (SOW).

I. Introduction

This project resulted from a request by the Smythe family of 1801 Brotherhood Avenue, Rockford, Pennsylvania. Although our primary focus is on weddings within the continental United States, this wedding will occur in Naples, Italy. This is GWI's first project outside the United States. It is expected that this project will lead to similar ones in the future, substantially increasing our revenues.

II. Scope

This project will require all our services provided for domestic weddings. These services include:

- Announcements, including to friends, relatives, and newspapers
- Ceremony and reception locations
- Decorations and props
- Entertainment
- Flowers
- Food and beverages
- Hotel accommodations
- Invitations
- Lighting
- Music
- Photography
- Prewedding parties and rehearsals, including bachelor parties and bridal showers
- Sound
- Travel
- Videotaping
- Wedding attire
- Wedding feast and cake
- Wedding transportation

Services required by the Smythes but not available through GWI will be contracted out.

III. Assumptions

The Smythe Project will be managed based on the following assumptions:

- Internal resources will be available to include electronic and staffing.
- Contracted services will perform when required.
- The project will have priority over existing projects.
- No legal problems will occur in holding a wedding outside the United States.

IV. Constraints

The following constraints will be placed on the project:

- Culture differences may impede performance.
- Resources must continue to support other wedding projects.

V. Performance Criteria

The project will comply with all requirements listed in the contract between the Smythe family and GWI. Any deviations from the contract must be reviewed by the steering committee and require signatures.

The project must finish on 11 June 2000. The cost for the wedding cannot exceed $1 million (U.S.).

VI. Product/Service Description

GWI will provide a full one-day wedding service on top of Mount Vesuvius on 11 June 2000. The wedding includes providing lodging for dignitaries, food, tourist attraction events, and entertainment. GWI will also arrange the wedding ceremony, feast, and itinerary for the honeymoon. Refer to the contract between the Smythe family and GWI. Also refer to Section II, Scope, for additional information.

VII. Major Responsibilities

The project manager will:

- Serve as the primary point of contact for the project.
- Develop and execute a comprehensive project plan.
- Keep the steering committee informed regarding progress.
- Use all resources efficiently and effectively.
- Evaluate changes to all baselines.

The steering committee will provide continuous overseeing for the project, which includes:

- Periodic review of progress
- Guidance and direction, when necessary
- Reporting to the internal customer

VIII. References

The primary documents supporting this statement of work are:

- Contract between GWI and the Smythe family
- Existing company policies and procedures

Exhibit 5-1. (Continued)

IX. Amendments

This document may be changed only after review and approval of first the steering committee and then the internal customer.

X. Signatures

- Project manager
- Steering committee members
- Internal customer

tity and quality. Recognizing such limitations early on enables realistic planning.

Performance Criteria

This section describes the criteria for customer satisfaction. Often, it points to three criteria: cost, schedule, and quality. The project cannot, for example, cost more than a set amount; specific milestones or red-letter dates must be met; service or product specifications must be addressed. This information allows for meaningful planning and ensures that the project will address key concerns.

Product/Service Description

This section has an overall description of the product or service. This description might include the basic features, characteristics, components, or deliverables to be produced. The content may be a narrative or a diagram. This information is useful for developing a work breakdown structure.

Major Responsibilities

This section delineates the high-level tasks of major participants. These tasks will be given in finer detail in the work breakdown structure.

References

This section lists any documentation that governs the content of the SOW. The documents often provide more details for planning.

Amendments

The SOW is not something etched in stone, contrary to popular belief. It is a living document that probably will be modified from time to time. This section is for appending any agreed-upon changes that come later.

Signatures

This section contains the approvals of all principal decision makers. At minimum, it should have signatures of the project manager, executive sponsor, customer, and executive steering committee members. If the ultimate customer is external to the company, as with the Smythe Project, the "customer" is frequently the liaison with the external customer. If this is the case, the statement of work usually becomes part of the terms and conditions of the formal contract.

Exhibit 5-2 shows a flowchart for developing a statement of work.

THE PROJECT ANNOUNCEMENT

With a completed SOW, Perry has one more task before he can start to plan: publishing a project announcement.

The project announcement is a widely distributed memo—albeit more than just another memo. It is also a way to give visibility to the proj-

Exhibit 5-2. Flowchart for statement of work.

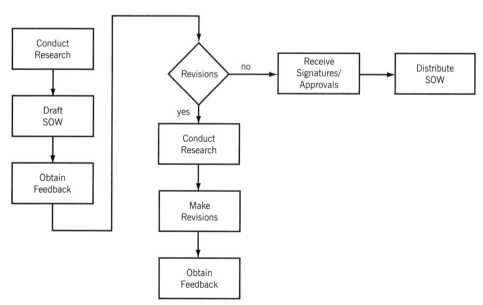

Exhibit 5-3. Project announcement.

Date: 15 January 2000
To: Jones, N., et al.
cc: Rogersby, H., et al.

Subject: Smythe Project

Perry Fitzberg has been designated the project manager for the Smythe Project. He will report directly to the executive steering committee, consisting of all functional vice-presidents of GWI.

The project must start no later than 30 January and be completed by 11 June 2000. The wedding will occur in Naples, Italy. Approximately 1,000 people will attend the event.

Amelia

Amelia Rainbow
President, GWI
Extension 3400
Mailstop 01-01

---

ect, communicate to everyone the priority of the project, and acquire the political muscle to compete with other projects.

The key question is, Who will prepare and sign the memo? Being a self-starter, Perry prepares the memo himself and presents it to Amelia for signature. He believes she is the internal customer and sponsor for the project. In many circumstances, however, there is a distinction between the two. Exhibit 5-3 shows the announcement.

With publication of the project announcement, Perry can begin planning. The planning function, as described in Chapter 1, entails many tasks, which are covered in Chapters 6 through 8.

Questions for Getting Started

1. Provide answers to these questions about your project:
   - What are the goals and objectives of the project?
   - Who are the principal participants?
   - When must the project be started and finished?

- Where will the project be executed?
- Why is the project being launched?
- How will the product or service be?

2. If you don't have the answers to any of the above, how are you going to get them?
    - By interview?
    - Document research?
    - Contact with the customer?

3. Is a statement of work, or understanding, necessary? If so, do you know what is contained in each of these sections:
    - Introduction?
    - Assumptions?
    - Constraints?
    - Performance criteria?
    - Product/service description?
    - Major responsibilities?
    - References?
    - Amendments?
    - Signatures?

4. Do you need a project announcement? If so, do you know:
    - Who will prepare it?
    - Who will sign it?
    - What the contents should be?

Chapter 6

The Work Breakdown Structure

Perry now has the visibility he needs and the details for building the project. Now he will use the SOW to develop a work breakdown structure, or WBS. The WBS is a detailed listing of the deliverables and tasks for building the product or delivering the service. It is a top-down, broad-to-specific hierarchical outcome of the work to perform.

There are several benefits to developing a WBS.

1. The WBS forces the project manager, team members, and customers to delineate the steps required to build and deliver the product or service. The exercise alone encourages a dialogue that will help clarify ambiguities, bring out assumptions, narrow the scope of the project, and raise critical issues early on.

2. It lays the groundwork for developing an effective schedule and good budget plans. A well-defined WBS enables resources to be allocated to specific tasks, helps in generating a meaningful schedule, and makes calculating a reliable budget easier.

3. The level of detail in a WBS makes it easier to hold people accountable for completing their tasks. With a defined WBS, people cannot hide under the "cover of broadness." A well-defined task can be assigned to a specific individual, who is then responsible for its completion.

4. The process of developing and completing a WBS breeds excitement and commitment. Although Perry will develop the high-level WBS, he will seek the participation of his core team to flesh out the WBS. This participation will spark involvement in the project.

Of course, developing a WBS is not easy. For one, it takes time—and plenty of it. A large WBS (one that identifies several thousand activities) can take several weeks to develop. For another, it requires effort. There is a knowledge transfer and exercise of brain power. The larger the scope of the project, the larger the WBS will be. More people must provide input

Where WBSs Go Wrong

More often than not, a simple WBS can improve the overall performance of a project. Sometimes, however, a WBS can do more harm than good. The reasons some WBSs fail are as follows:

1. The WBS does not have sufficient detail. If it is kept to too high a level, estimating, and tracking the schedule and cost performance become "guesstimation." Composite or roll-up views lack meaning because the lower-level content is missing or too general to be reliable.

2. The WBS is the result of one individual and does not include those who will work on the tasks. When the WBS is published, few team members have a sense of ownership or commitment to the contents.

3. The WBS does not cover the whole project. It contains only the activities needed to build the project. It might omit other important activities, such as project administration and training. The result is that subsequent delivery of the product or service is unsatisfactory.

4. The entire WBS is not used in subsequent planning. The project manager takes an eclectic view of the WBS, using only selected portions. The result is incomplete planning, lacking a comprehensive view of the work to be done.

5. There is a failure to put the WBS under configuration management. Once everyone agrees on its contents, the WBS should not become "frozen" or "baselined," with all future changes not identified or evaluated for their impact on the project. Failure to manage changes to the WBS can result in unanticipated impacts on the scope, schedule, or cost.

and then approve the portion they are responsible to perform. Finally, the WBS requires continual refinement. The first iteration is rarely right and as the project changes, so does the WBS. Still, the advantages outweigh the challenges. A good WBS makes planning and executing a project easier.

As Perry progresses down each leg of the WBS, he gets to a level of detail that provides the ability to track and monitor progress, make assignments that build accountability, and reliably estimate the hours to perform tasks. How detailed the WBS gets depends on the level of control the project manager wants. Generally, the more specific the WBS, the more accurate the planning and the greater the ability to monitor progress. A common heuristic Perry uses is the 80-hour rule: each of the lowest-level items in the WBS should not exceed 80 hours' effort. If the job requires more, then he breaks down the task into smaller tasks. Perry recognizes that he will have to continually refine the WBS as he estimates the time to complete tasks.

To begin developing a WBS, Perry identifies all the requirements for the wedding. First he reviews the SOW, which provides a guideline since it is representative of a high level and contains all the necessary information. Other sources of information for building the WBS are documentation, including the WBS, of related projects; interview notes; legal documentation; and memorandums.

With this information, Perry decides on how to approach the WBS. There are many ways to draw up a WBS—for example, by responsibility (see Exhibit 6-1); by phase; or by deliverables. He decides on deliverables for this WBS since that worked best for him in the past. It is also easier to determine progress at a higher level when reporting to senior management or the customer.

Exhibit 6-1. Work breakdown structure based on responsibility.

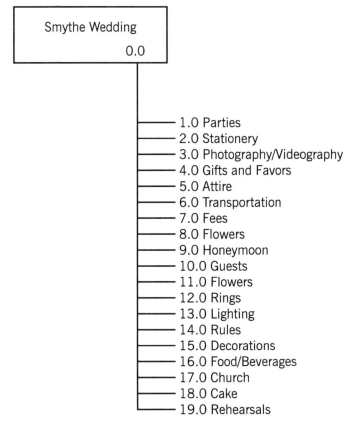

Smythe Wedding
0.0

- 1.0 Parties
- 2.0 Stationery
- 3.0 Photography/Videography
- 4.0 Gifts and Favors
- 5.0 Attire
- 6.0 Transportation
- 7.0 Fees
- 8.0 Flowers
- 9.0 Honeymoon
- 10.0 Guests
- 11.0 Flowers
- 12.0 Rings
- 13.0 Lighting
- 14.0 Rules
- 15.0 Decorations
- 16.0 Food/Beverages
- 17.0 Church
- 18.0 Cake
- 19.0 Rehearsals

The WBS generally consists of two components. The first component is the product breakdown structure (PBS), which delineates the segments that constitute the final product or service. It may also contain items deemed important (e.g., training). Each item in the PBS is described with a noun and a unique number.

The other component is the task breakdown structure (TBS), which contains the tasks to build or deliver something (see Exhibit 6-2). It may also list tasks deemed important to the project. Each task in the TBS is described with an action verb, a noun, and a unique number.

The lowest level in the WBS is the *work package level.* These are the tasks or subtasks he will use to assign responsibilities, construct schedules, and track progress. Consider the WBS as a giant topical outline. Each level lower is a breakdown of a higher level. The items in the lower level constitute the one in the next higher level. Sometimes the higher levels of a WBS are managerial levels; the details are "rolled up" to the managerial level for reporting purposes. Lower levels are called technical levels.

Exhibit 6-2. Task breakdown structure (TBS).

Smythe Wedding
0.0

6.0 Transportation

6.1 Wedding
6.1.1 Bride and groom
6.1.1.1 Identify limousine service to church
6.1.1.2 Coordinate limousine service to church
6.1.1.3 Identify limousine service to reception
6.1.1.4 Coordinate limousine service to reception

6.1.2 Guests
6.1.2.1 Determine transportation requirements to church
6.1.2.2 Coordinate transportation to church
6.1.2.3 Determine transportation requirements to and from reception
6.1.2.4 Coordinate transportation requirements to and from reception
6.1.2.5 Arrange for valet service for church
6.1.2.6 Arrange for valet service for reception

On very large projects, each task in the work package has an accompanying description, contained in a WBS dictionary. Each entry in the dictionary describes the expected output of the task. Thus, a WBS dictionary can help the project manager determine whether a task has been completed.

Perry's WBS for the Smythe wedding is shown in the Appendix. He used a word processing program to produce it. But he can also display the WBS graphically, as a tree diagram, by using graphics software. Another way is to post sticky notes on a wall to display the hierarchical relationship. Either way, the display will look like Exhibit 6-3.

With his draft of the WBS ready, Perry is now able to solicit input from the key players. He presents it to the steering committee and obtains their acceptance. Next, he identifies the key skills needed to perform the tasks and obtains additional input from team members. The PBS gives him an idea of the following needed expertise:

- Attendants
- Cosmetologist
- Drivers
- Florist
- Hair stylist

Exhibit 6-3. Graphic display of task breakdown structure.

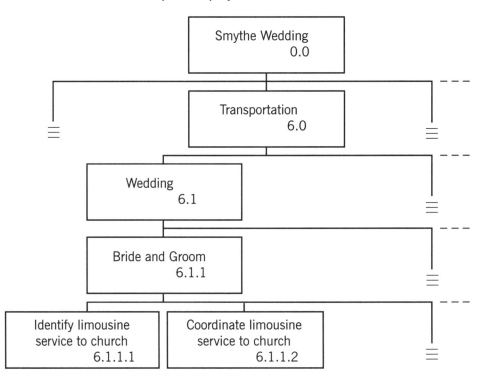

- Jewelers
- Lawyer
- Musicians
- Photographer
- Planners
- Public relations expert
- Receptionists
- Tailor
- Travel agents
- Ushers
- Valet
- Videographer
- Waiters
- Wedding consultants

At the moment, Perry has no idea how many people with the requisite expertise are necessary. But he will require at least one of each on the core team (the key participants).

To acquire core team members, Perry needs once again to present his case to the steering committee, and upon receiving its approval, to contact the relevant functional organizations. Perry now has his core team, as shown in Exhibit 6-4. Perry then solicits input from these core team members regarding the WBS and gets ready to take on the next step in planning: estimating the time to complete each task.

The work breakdown structure, although time-consuming to prepare, is an excellent foundation for the remaining project planning functions. Next we consider the work-time estimates; which aid in the preparation of schedules and costs.

Questions for Getting Started

1. What are the deliverables for your project? Did you display them in the product breakdown structure (PBS) of the WBS?

Exhibit 6-4. Core team members.

Attendant, Pat Jones	Public relations expert, Eva Brewster
Cosmetologist, Cynthia Fralusinski	Receptionist, Wonda Wrangell
Driver, Terry Karla	Tailor, Frank Galucci
Florist, David Rockford	Travel agent, Larry Eisenberg
Jeweler, Henry Winkless	Usher, Michael Cramer
Lawyer, Robin Schister	Valet, Danny Smith
Musician, Vy Toon	Videographer, Raymond Leazowitz
Photographer, Gina Davies	Waiter, Ted Rogers
Planner, Hank Wilson	Wedding consultant, Mary Ewing

2. What are the tasks for your project? Did you display them in the task breakdown structure (TBS) of the WBS?
3. Did you receive input from all relevant parties when building the WBS?
4. Did you perform the following when building the WBS:
    - Explode each leg down to the lowest level of detail (e.g., using the 80-hour rule)?
    - Give each item a unique number?
    - Give each item in the PBS a name consisting of an adjective and a noun?
    - Give each item in the TBS a name consisting of an action verb and an object?
5. Did you put the WBS under configuration control in the event that an item is added, removed, or modified?

Chapter 7
Techniques for Estimating Work Times

With the work breakdown structure complete, Perry can now estimate the time required to complete each task. But remember, an estimate is just that, an estimate. The best Perry or any project manager can hope to develop are reliable estimates—ones that offer confidence in being achievable.

THE BENEFITS AND CHALLENGES OF ESTIMATING WORK TIMES

Estimating the work times provides several benefits for the project manager. It gives an idea of the level of effort required to complete a project. This information then enables the project manager to produce a realistic plan based upon that effort. Estimating also helps the project manager anticipate the budget for the project. Allocated funds are largely based on the effort, or labor, to produce the product or deliver the service.

The estimate becomes the basis for developing a schedule. Hours are converted to flow time, which in turn is used, with the interrelationships among tasks, to calculate start and stop dates. Lastly, doing an estimate breeds commitment. If the people who will do the work also help make the estimates, they will feel more committed to their tasks and keep within the allotted time.

While it offers many benefits, estimating is not easy, for two reasons. First, it takes time and effort to develop reliable estimates. Many people take the path of least resistance and generate either an extremely pessimistic or an overly optimistic estimate. Good estimating requires extensive calculation and research to avoid skewing the calculated values. Second, estimating requires dealing with ambiguity. By its very nature, estimating has both knowns and unknowns. The unknowns can generate fear or cause people to react out of ignorance. Either way, confidence in the resulting estimate is low.

TYPES OF ESTIMATING TECHNIQUES

Perry and his team can use one of four techniques to estimate the time it will take to complete each task:

1. Scientific wildly assumed guess
2. Global efficiency factor
3. Productivity adjustment percent
4. Program evaluation and review, or three-point estimating, technique

Scientific Wildly Assumed Guess (SWAG)

This technique is the most popular, yet the most unreliable. The SWAG is most popular because it is quick. The estimator determines a single value for time to do the work; no long calculations are necessary. The estimator provides one figure for each task, quickly. The SWAG is also popular because it requires very little research. Often, one or two individuals can do the entire estimate. It is rarely based on in-depth analysis to derive the values.

However, the SWAG is also very unreliable for two reasons. First, it is highly subjective, based on one person's estimate of doing a task. It accounts for only a limited number of factors, relying on an hour estimate that is based on a "feel" for doing the work.

Second, it understates or overinflates the time. If the estimators hold themselves in high regard, then the estimate will be optimistic; if they lack confidence, then it will be pessimistic. As long as the same people do the same work, then the estimates may prove reliable. What happens, though, if someone does the work who had no input to the estimate? What happens if an obstacle arises that the new person cannot handle? Then the estimate becomes unreliable.

For these two reasons alone, Perry decides not to use the SWAG technique. Now he is thinking about using the global efficiency factor technique.

Global Efficiency Factor (GEF)

This technique is also easy to use and attempts to incorporate nonproductive time into the estimate. The estimation assumes that a person is 100 percent productive. Then the estimator accounts for nonproductive factors that are each assigned a percent relative to each other. The estimator deducts the percents from 100 percent to derive a more realistic estimate, as follows:

Task 10.4 Arrange for food and beverage

Deficiency	Percent to Deduct
Unsatisfactory skill level	8
Unfamiliarity with project	10
Unfamiliarity with tools	5
Lack of well-defined requirements	2
Total Deficiency	25

Estimate to perform work   100 hours
Adjusted estimate   125 hours [100 hours + (100 hours × 25%)]

The GEF is not as popular but it does have its adherents. They believe that it accounts for nonproductive time and eliminates the tendency toward unwarranted optimism.

However, the GEF technique has its drawbacks. The percents to deduct are often subjective themselves, thereby skewed and subjective. The percent for each deduction will also often vary among people. Perry decides, therefore, to look at another estimating technique: the productivity adjustment percent.

Productivity Adjustment Percent (PAP)

The PAP technique attempts to do on a more global scale what the GEF does. It applies an overall productivity factor to the estimate for all tasks. For our example, we assume people are 80 percent productive:

Task 8.2.1 Determine floral requirements

100% − 80% = 20%. We now add this 20% factor to our baseline of 100%, giving us a PAP of 120%, or 1.2.

Estimate to perform work   100 hours
Adjusted estimate   120 hours (100 hours × 1.20)

The PAP has its adherents, for two reasons. First, it is based on historical figures. Work measurement studies are frequently used to derive the overall percent. Second, it is easy to apply this calculation. There are no percent deductions on a task-by-task basis nor any burdensome mathematical calculations.

Despite these two benefits, there are some disadvantages. The historical records are not always available to determine the productivity factor for an organization. Also, the figure is so global that it may not be relevant to a specific task. Finally, it does not account for the complexity of issues involving individual tasks. For these three reasons, Perry does not use the PAP technique. That leaves one other option: the PERT.

Program Evaluation and Review Technique (PERT)

The PERT, also known as the three-point estimating technique, uses three estimates of time to complete a task. The three estimates are the most likely, most pessimistic, and most optimistic. The most likely time is the effort (usually in hours) to complete a task under normal or reasonable conditions. The most pessimistic time is the effort to complete a task under the worst conceivable circumstances. The most optimistic is the effort to complete a task under the best or ideal circumstances. The three variables are then used to calculate an expected time to complete a task, as shown below:

$$\text{Expected time} = \frac{\text{Most optimistic} + (4 \times \text{most likely}) + \text{most pessimistic}}{6}$$

Task 1.3.2.1 Determine type of entertainment/music

$$\text{Expected time} = \frac{18 + (4 \times 72) + 100}{6} = \frac{406}{6} = 67.7 \text{ hours}$$

This estimating technique accounts for the level of effort to complete a task after accounting for all the parameters to do the work. The estimator assumes that a person is 100 percent productive during the time to complete the task. Realistically, of course, no one is 100 percent productive. Some time is inevitably spent being nonproductive, so the hour estimates are adjusted to account for this nonproductive time (e.g., telephone calls, meetings, break times). This time has no direct relationship to the work being done; the results have no impact on progress on the actual work. Below is an example of how to calculate the revised expected time:

Task 10.3 Coordinate transportation (ground and air)

Estimate to perform work = 500 hours
500 hours × 1.10 (for 10% nonproductive time) = 550 hours
Revised expected time = 550 hours

The three-point estimating technique has its problems. For one, it is time consuming; performing the calculations can take a long time, even when a computer is used, especially for a large project. Also, it is laborious; performing the calculations requires considerable thinking and searching for reliable information. Lastly, not too many people understand the rea-

---

How to Reevaluate an Estimate

Sometimes you might feel uncomfortable with an estimate. Perhaps you suspect it is unrealistic. Perhaps you think the reasoning behind it is faulty. Perhaps you do not trust the people making the estimate. Whatever the reason, you can take several actions to validate the estimate.

You can check the historical records of other projects that dealt with similar work. Sometimes, however, such data are either difficult to obtain or unavailable.

You can seek a second opinion. It might mean going to someone on another project where similar work was performed. It might mean going to an outside expert or organization for an evaluation.

You can benchmark one or more tasks. It may mean comparing the estimates with similar ongoing or completed projects, either inside or outside your company.

You can apply the Delphi approach. Simply identify a number of people to provide input on an estimate. Then make the adjustment and resubmit the estimate to them for further adjustment. The adjustment ends once you gain concurrence or are comfortable with the result.

Finally, you can conduct peer reviews. Once all the estimates are complete, you can assemble everyone in a room to discuss the estimate for each task. Assumptions and issues may arise that will call into question the validity of some estimates. New estimates can then be developed.

---

sons for taking this approach; its underpinnings are probability and bell curve analysis, which can be intimidating and too academic for some people.

The technique, however, does offer four benefits. It forces people to think seriously about the time to complete a task; the three variables require looking at as many parameters as possible to calculate a realistic estimate. The estimate is more reliable than other estimating techniques; it accounts for many parameters to compensate for being too optimistic or pessimistic. It improves communication; discussion over the parameters that relate to each variable forces people to communicate to come to a conclusion. It identifies issues and assumptions early. When calculating each variable, people must identify issues and assumptions. To ignore issues and assumptions adds to the cost of addressing them later in the project cycle.

What Happens When No One Wants to Give the Project Manager an Estimate?

Project managers often lack formal authority over the people on their teams. This is especially the case in a matrix environment, where people report to a functional manager and may support several projects simultaneously.

Sometimes project managers just do not get cooperation from team members. The team members may fear commiting themselves, hate to wrestle with unknowns or ambiguities, or just not like the project manager. What, then, is a project manager to do?

Project managers have several options:

1. They can document the refusal to cooperate in a memo and address it to the functional manager. This takes advantage of formal authority to get the estimate.

2. They can hold a team meeting, where everyone can discuss and share their estimates in the presence of other team members. This takes advantage of peer pressure to get the estimate.

3. They can solicit input from other people. Then they present the estimate to the uncooperative team member and formally request his or her feedback. This takes advantage of professional pride.

4. They can make the estimate themselves and inform the person in a memo that unless there is acceptance by a certain date, the accuracy of the estimate will be assumed. This takes advantage of time pressure.

Of the four estimating techniques, Perry elects the three-point estimating technique. He believes that it will provide more-reliable estimates and also offer many other benefits. So, using the three-point estimating technique requires Perry to keep in mind the following points.

1. He must get input estimates from the people who will do the actual work. He appreciates their knowledge of what is required to complete the work. He also knows that getting their input will encourage commitment to their assigned tasks. It is one thing to follow someone's dictate of the hours to do the work; it is another when he does the estimate himself.

2. He must look at the historical records of other projects. Rather than apply the estimating technique for all tasks, he may uncover some

reliable estimates that can be reused for similar tasks. He is cautious enough to realize that circumstances are not always exactly the same from one project to another. Consequently, the reusable estimate may require revision. Also, he reminds himself that it is still a good idea to get input from people who will do the work.

3. He must identify and document the assumptions and parameters used to derive the estimates. Doing this is important for two reasons. First, he and others will better understand the rationale behind the estimates. Second, he can also determine what has changed since making the estimate and make revisions accordingly.

4. He must maintain consistency in the estimating process. He avoids using the three-point estimate technique for some tasks and not for others. Otherwise, he will mix "apples with oranges," with some estimates being realistic, optimistic, or pessimistic. A lack of discipline in this regard can result in an unrealistic schedule.

5. He must make the estimates public. After getting feedback, he will publish the estimates. He does not hide the estimates, as though they were his personal golf scores or bowling averages. By publishing the estimates, Perry knows that people will feel a subtle pressure to use them.

6. He must understand that the estimates are approximations, not accuracies. Circumstances change that make estimates irrelevant. That requires reestimating during the project to increase the reliability and validity of the overall estimate. Ideally, an estimate has the highest confidence level, which becomes more possible as a project progresses through its cycle.

FACTORS TO CONSIDER IN DRAWING UP ESTIMATES

Estimators consider many factors when performing their calculations. These include:

- Availability of nonlabor support
- Clarity and definitiveness of scope
- Complexity of the work
- Degree of available information to estimate
- Degree of uncertainty or risk in achieving the outcome
- Experience, knowledge, and expertise of the team members
- Financial constraints on the project
- History of similar work performed
- Legal constraints on the project
- Location of team members working on the task
- Number of people assigned to the task

- Number of potential interruptions
- Priority of the task
- Productivity of team members
- Project size
- Standardization of processes related to the task
- Structure versus unstructured nature of the work to be performed
- Whether the completion date of the task is dictated

When estimating, Perry will consider Parkinson's law. He knows that too much available time to perform a task is almost as troublesome as too little. Parkinson's law, of course, says that work expands to fill the time available. In other words, if given ten hours to complete a task when it ordinarily takes five hours, people will take ten hours. So Perry treats Parkinson's law seriously.

Perry is now ready for the next big planning action: developing a schedule.

Questions for Getting Started

1. Did you identify all the work package items in the work breakdown structure?
2. Did you select the most appropriate estimating technique? What are the reasons for your choice?
3. With at least the core team members, did you get time estimates for the tasks they are responsible for completing?
4. If you meet resistance, how do you plan to overcome it?
5. If necessary, how will you reevaluate estimates? Review historical records? Apply the Delphi approach?

Chapter 8

Schedule Development and the Network Diagram

With the statement of work and the work estimates completed, Perry is now ready to do some scheduling. In so doing, he will juggle six factors: scope, time, duration, tasks, logic, and resources. The *scope* is described in the SOW. *Time* is the hour estimate to complete each task—in other words, the estimates. *Duration* is the hour figure converted to flow time for completing each task and, consequently, the entire project. *Tasks* are the entries in the WBS. *Logic* is the sequence of tasks. And *resources* are the labor and nonlabor investments assigned to each task. But all of this will become clearer as we explain more about scheduling.

WHAT SCHEDULING IS

Scheduling entails making a logical sequence of tasks and then calculating start and stop dates for each task. The results are displayed as a diagram.

A schedule is only useful if people are willing to commit themselves to maintaining it. Therefore, Perry sits down with his core team and determines the logical sequence of tasks. He has everyone look at the big picture, tying together all the tasks. They use this perspective to draw a *network diagram,* like the one in Exhibit 8-1. The network diagram displays the logical relationships between the tasks.

Network diagramming may initially seem complex, especially if you've not had previous experience drawing flowcharts. The advantages, however, are great. By constructing the diagram, you focus on the project goal and discover the appropriate approach. Difficult issues become apparent, so the effort and expense of dealing with them later is avoided. In addition, the diagram enables easier tracking of performance because it is based on the work-package level items in the WBS. Finally, making forecasts and "what-if" scenarios is easier.

Warning Signs of Bad Scheduling Practices

Bad scheduling practices can tarnish the credibility of a schedule. Watch for these two common indicators of bad scheduling:

- *Warning Sign Number 1:* Sometimes people are unsure of the future, so rather than calculate an end date for a task, they write "TBD," or "to be determined." It not only represents unclear and incomplete thinking but also opens the opportunity for guesswork and poor oversight of tasks.
- *Warning Sign Number 2:* Occasionally people will develop schedules that contain too much negative float (being too tight) or too much positive float (being too loose). Either way, it indicates a problem with the schedule, especially one of realism. Too much negative float indicates that the schedule cannot be realistically accomplished; too much positive float indicates that estimates for the tasks are too low.

TASK DEPENDENCIES AND DATE SCHEDULING

A network diagram will show one or more of the following relationships, or dependencies, between tasks.

Finish-to-Start

An earlier activity, or the predecessor, is completed and the next one, the successor, is begun, as illustrated in Exhibit 8-2. Sometimes the suc-

Exhibit 8-1. Network diagram.

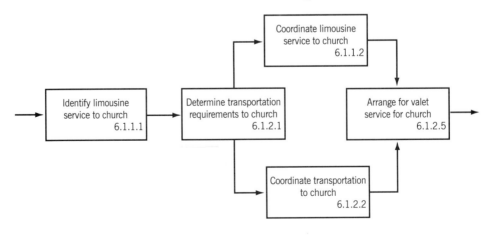

Exhibit 8-2. Finish-to-start relationship.

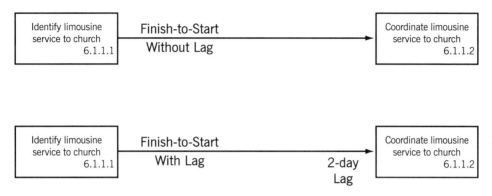

ceeding task is not begun immediately; there is, in other words, a lapse of time between the end of the predecessor and the start of the successor. That interval is called lag. A task can have one or more predecessors or successors.

Start-to-Start

Two activities are begun around the same time, as displayed in Exhibit 8-3. Sometimes one task is begun just a little later than the other; the gap between the start of one task and the beginning of the other is also called lag.

Finish-to-Finish

Two activities are finished around the same time, as shown in Exhibit 8-4. Sometimes one task will finish earlier than the other, yet each must finish before its successor is begun. The time between the finish of one and the other is also called lag.

Exhibit 8-3. Start-to-start relationship.

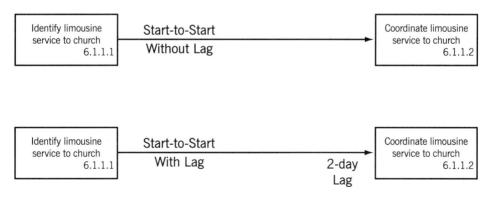

Exhibit 8-4. Finish-to-finish relationship.

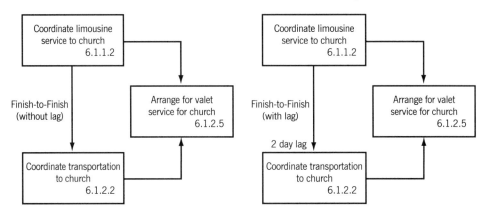

Having identified all the dependencies between the tasks, Perry can apply the time estimates to each task. But the raw time estimates must be converted to some meaningful value. For starting purposes only, Perry converts the hour estimates into workdays. He divides the hours by 8 to derive the number of days needed to complete the task. He then uses this *duration,* or flow time, to calculate the start and stop date for each task.

Actually, Perry calculates two sets of start and stop dates: early and late start dates, and early and late finish dates. The early start and early finish dates are the first pair to calculate. The early start date is the earliest time a task can be begun. The early finish date is the earliest time a task can be

---

Why Some People Don't Do Scheduling

Occasionally you run into people who do not like schedules. Sometimes that person is even the project manager.

There are all sorts of reasons for this reluctance. People might feel the time or effort expended to build the schedule exceeds the value gained. Or they might not want to commit themselves.

If you are working with someone who is reluctant to schedule, you have several options. You can document a person's reluctance in a memo and send it to higher-level management. You can hold a group meeting and cover the schedule in general, letting peer pressure prompt the person to cooperate. A related tactic is to apply the Delphi method by encouraging input from everyone, then make changes, recirculate for feedback, and repeat the cycle until everyone is satisfied with the results.

completed. These dates are determined by comparing the duration of a task with the dates for the preceding and succeeding tasks.

Some dates may not be logically derived from a network diagram. For example, certain tasks may have to start no earlier than a specific date or may not finish earlier or later than a specific time. In some cases, tasks may have to begin or finish on a specified date; these are known as *constraint dates.* Likewise, the start or finish date of a task may depend on the start or completion of a task in another project. The output of one project, for example, may feed another. Under these circumstances, the task has an external dependency that must be considered when calculating start and finish dates.

PERRY'S SCHEDULING METHOD

Here's how Perry calculates the early start and early finish dates for his tasks. First, he assigns activity numbers to the tasks in the WBS and converts the time estimates into flow times, as shown below:

Activity Number	Task Description	Hours	Duration (Hours/8)
6.1.1.1	Identify limousine service to church	24	3
6.1.1.2	Coordinate limousine service to church	8	1
6.1.2.1	Determine transportation requirements to church	24	3
6.1.2.2	Coordinate transportation to church	16	2
6.1.2.5	Arrange for valet service for church	8	1

Next, Perry logically ties all the tasks together in a network diagram. (A network diagram was shown in Exhibit 8-1.) After determining the durations and sequences, Perry calculates the early start and early finish dates for each task and then the entire project. He performs the *forward pass,* by moving from the first task in the network diagram up through the last.

Now, as shown in Exhibit 8-5, Perry knows that task 6.1.1.1 will begin on 8:00 A.M., April 1. He also knows that the previous task was completed the day before. He knows, too, that the duration is three days, meaning the task will be done on April 1, 2, and 3, finishing at 5:00 P.M. on the April 3. Task 6.1.2.1 is the successor and it will begin on April 4 at 8:00 A.M. It, too, has a duration of three days and is completed at 5:00 P.M. on April 6.

Two successor tasks follow 6.1.2.1. They both will begin on the day after 6.1.2.1 is completed, April 7. Task 6.1.2.2 has a duration of two days,

Exhibit 8-5. Forward pass (where ES is early start, EF is early finish).

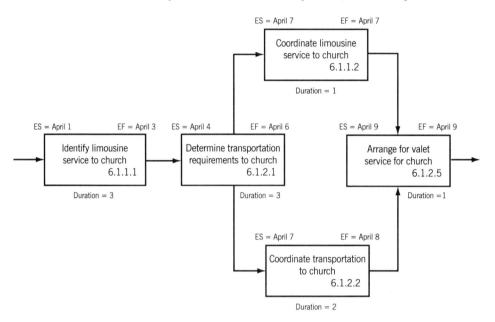

so it is completed at 5:00 P.M. on April 8. Task 6.1.1.2 has a duration of one day, so its completion date is April 7.

Task 6.1.2.5 cannot be begun until its two predecessor tasks are finished. The one that is finished the furthest out—6.1.2.2—must end before 6.1.2.5 can begin. Hence, 6.1.2.5 will begin on April 9 and, with a duration of one day, will be completed on April 9.

Perry now calculates the late start and late finish dates for each task. Using the same durations and dependencies in the network diagram, he moves from right to left, beginning with the very last task and calculating the late start and late finish dates. This movement from right to left is the *backward pass,* as shown in Exhibit 8-6.

Assuming that the finish date to task 6.1.2.5 has been set as April 9, Perry can begin the backward pass. He knows that 6.1.2.5 has a duration of one day and, consequently, begins on that same day, providing a late start date of April 9. He realizes that task 6.1.2.5 has two predecessors, 6.1.1.2 and 6.1.2.2. Since they each finish the day before, their late finish dates are April 8. Task 6.1.2.2 has a duration of two days and, consequently, has a late start date of April 7. Since task 6.1.1.2 is a concurrent activity, and has a shorter duration, it can begin as far back as April 7, the same late start date as 6.1.2.2. Since 6.1.2.1 is the predecessor to both 6.1.1.2 and 6.1.2.2, it must have a late finish date of April 6. Since task 6.1.2.1's duration is three days, its late start date is April 4. And since task 6.1.1.1 is the predecessor of 6.1.2.1, it must finish the day before, on April 3; with a duration of three days, it must have a late start on April 1.

Is Work Group Participation the Best Way?

In many environments, project managers develop schedules without input or feedback from the people who will be doing the work. There are several reasons for this.

One is the time required to obtain this input. Getting people involved adds time, and the more people, the more time to develop the schedule. Also, the project manager has overall responsibility for the project. The project manager has the big picture perspective and can ensure that "all the pieces fit together."

The counterargument is that the work group should have a say in building the schedule. Although participation adds to the flow time, it does offer some powerful advantages. By obtaining input, the project manager solicits ownership in and commitment to the schedule, especially for the work each person is responsible to do. Work group participation also helps to raise issues and question assumptions early to preclude future misunderstandings and problems.

Exhibit 8-6. Backward pass (where LS is late start, LF is late finish).

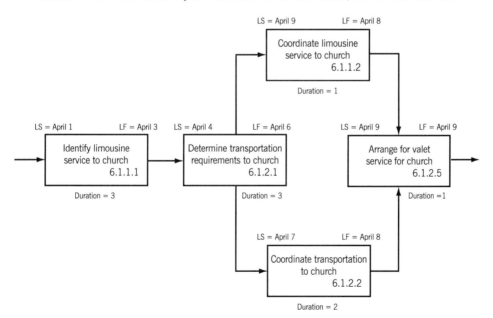

Note: this is only a partial description of the network diagram for the wedding. It's a "snapshot" presented here to illustrate the basics of network diagramming and calculating dates.

THE FLOAT

Perry now has four dates for each task: early start, early finish, late start, and late finish. These dates are necessary to calculate the float for a task. *Float* is the time an activity can slide without affecting the project completion date. For instance, if a task does not have to be begun right away, there may be time to slide. Or if it does not have to be finished as early as possible, there is time to let the date slide a bit.

Perry uses a simple calculation to determine float: the difference between the early start date and the late finish date, minus the duration, as shown in Exhibit 8-7.

Tasks given a zero float means that they cannot slide; if they do, then the project end date will slide, too. The one or more paths through the network diagram that have tasks with zero floats are called the *critical path*, as shown in Exhibit 8-7.

There are, in reality, two types of float. The float just described is known as *total float* and affects the project end date. The other type is the

Exhibit 8-7. Critical path showing float.

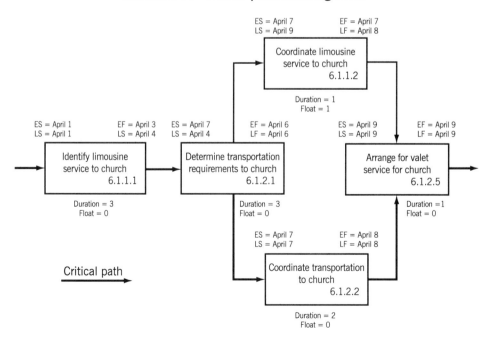

free float, which occurs on noncritical paths. This is the time that an activity can slide without impacting the start date of its successor.

OTHER TYPES OF NETWORK DIAGRAMS

Perry has used one type of network diagram, but several other types exist. Perry's choice is the *precedence diagramming method.* It is used most often in nonconstruction applications, such as in the information systems, pharmaceutical, and engineering industries.

For construction applications, the *arrow diagramming method* is used. It, too, relies on relationships, but they take a different form. The arrow diagram uses "nodes" to represent events and arrows to describe the task between those nodes. Also, this technique uses dummy activities that consume no resources, unlike the precedence diagramming method.

Another diagramming technique is the *bar,* or *Gantt, chart.* The fundamental difference between a bar chart and a network diagram is that the former does not show dependencies. The bar chart displays a list of tasks and, for each one, a bar shows the flow time or duration. As Exhibit 8-8 shows, a standard bar chart does not present all four dates for a task.

The bar chart often is useful, for several reasons. It is easy to read, showing only one set of start and finish dates. The bar itself provides a visual means to check the status of a task. It is also excellent for "rolling up," or summarizing the progress of a related group of tasks. Thus, its simplicity, visual orientation, and summarization capabilities make it an excellent tool for reporting to senior management. It gives senior management the big picture rather than the details. A bar chart using roll-ups is shown in Exhibit 8-9.

Exhibit 8-8. Basic bar chart.

Task	Duration	April			
		Week 1	Week 2	Week 3	Week 4
6.1.1.1 Identify limousine service to church	3	▭			
6.1.2.1 Determine transportation requirements to church	3	▭			
6.1.1.2 Coordinate limousine service to church	1		▯		
6.1.2.2 Coordinate transportation to church	2		▭		
6.1.2.5 Arrange for valet service for church	1		▯		

Exhibit 8-9. Roll-up bar chart.

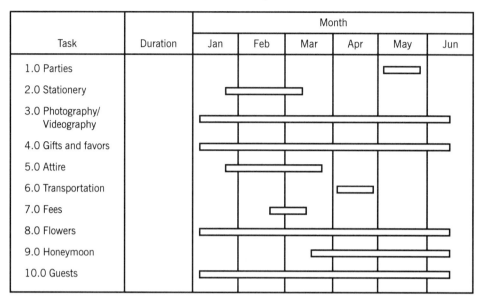

The milestone chart is a type of bar chart. It has the outlay of a bar chart but also has an icon or symbol to mark the occurrence of an event. The icon has a duration of zero. This event might be receiving approval or the completion of a task. Exhibit 8-10 is an example of a milestone chart. Like the basic bar chart, it is best used when reporting to senior management.

Exhibit 8-10. Milestone chart.

Task	Duration	Jan	Feb	Mar	Apr	May	Jun
				Month			
1.0 Parties						◊	
2.0 Stationery				◊			
3.0 Photography/ Videography							◊
4.0 Gifts and favors							◊
5.0 Attire				◊			
6.0 Transportation					◊		
7.0 Fees				◊			
8.0 Flowers							◊
9.0 Honeymoon							◊
10.0 Guests							◊

Perry uses the network diagram to plan the details of the project and manage it from day to day. He uses the bar chart for reporting to senior management.

THE SCHEDULE AS A ROAD MAP

Using the work breakdown structure and the time estimates that he developed earlier, Perry builds a realistic schedule. The schedule provides a road map for him and all team members to follow.

However, he realizes that a schedule can help him to accomplish only so much. He also needs to organize his project so that he can efficiently and effectively execute his plan.

Questions for Getting Started

1. Did you develop a network diagram or a bar chart? Or both?
2. If you developed a network diagram, did you:
   - Assign task numbers to each item in the WBS? Is the numbering scheme meaningful?
   - Identify the people who will help you put the logic together?
   - Tie all the tasks together to form a complete, logical diagram?
   - Convert the hours for each task to flow time or duration?
   - Calculate the early and late start and finish dates for each task?
   - Consider the constraints, such as imposed dates, when calculating dates?
   - Consider relationship types and lag?
   - Calculate float to identify the critical path(s)?
   - Obtain all core team members' concurrence?

Chapter 9

Resource Allocation: Aligning People and Other Resources With Tasks

For the Smythe Project to succeed, Perry must have sufficient resources—that is, both people and things—and use them efficiently and effectively. Resource allocation, a part of the organizing function, allows him to do that.

As Perry knows, a project manager has a wide variety of resources to employ, including people, supplies, equipment, and facilities. People, for most projects in general and for the Smythe Project in particular, are the predominant resource and, consequently, the major focus here to illustrate resource allocation principles.

Resource allocation involves four basic steps:

1. IDENTIFY THE TASKS INVOLVED

Perry goes directly to the network diagram to identify the tasks involved in his project. These tasks are the same ones as at the work package level in the work breakdown structure (see Chapter 6).

2. ASSIGN RESOURCES TO THOSE TASKS

Perry starts determining how to best apply his resources. When assigning people resources, he considers several factors, including:

- Availability
- Available budget
- Education/training
- Equipment to do work

- Expertise
- Individual's desire or interest
- Knowledge
- Personality
- Teaming

Perry also considers behavioral factors, such as personality. He recognizes that some people may not be suitable to do certain tasks (e.g., an engineer may well be unsuitable to do the work of a salesman).

Perry also considers the motivational tools at his disposal. He will use job enlargement, for instance, to challenge certain people to assume more responsibilities. He uses job enrichment to motivate other team members. And he considers job rotation. Of course, Perry recognizes that there are some risks, mainly the inability of the person to handle different or greater responsibilities. However, Perry is willing to take the chance in applying his people resources, since the potential payback in productivity will easily outweigh the risks.

When allocating resources, Perry applies the following heuristics (or rules of thumb):

- With noncritical tasks, give preference to the task with the least float.
- Give priority to tasks on the critical path.
- If two activities are critical and have the same float, give preference to the more complex task.

3. BUILD A RESOURCE PROFILE

The resource profile graphically displays the planned and actual use of one or more resources over the duration of a task, group of tasks, or entire project. The display is often a histogram, as shown in Exhibit 9-1. The x-axis shows a time continuum reflecting the early or late start and finish dates. The y-axis shows the cumulative hours to perform one or more tasks. The continuous vertical bars profile the cumulative hours that someone will work on one or more concurrent tasks.

The initial histogram often has an irregular shape. The high points are peaks, reflecting greater use of resources at a specific point in time. The low points are valleys, reflecting lower use of resources at a specific point in time. Exhibit 9-1 is an example of a histogram with several peaks and valleys.

An irregular shape to the histogram reflects that resources are being employed inefficiently or ineffectively. The peaks may indicate that the schedule is too tight (i.e., compressed durations), thereby requiring extensive overtime to complete the work. The schedule may be too loose (i.e.,

Exhibit 9-1. Unleveled histogram.

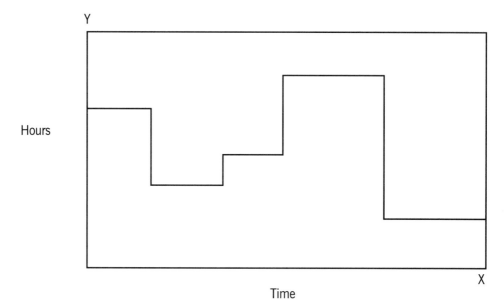

durations too spread out). The valleys may indicate that too much time is available to complete a task. Either way, such scenarios can negatively affect motivation, performance, and productivity. Too much duration communicates a lack of importance or urgency. Too little duration can lead to burnout, negative conflict, and work owing to oversights or mistakes.

Therefore, Perry attempts to reduce the number of peaks and valleys by smoothing out the histogram as much as possible, similar to what appears in Exhibit 9-2. The result is called a *leveled* histogram, and the process of smoothing it out is called level loading. Of course, a histogram is rarely flat.

4. Adjust the Schedule or Pursue Alternatives

Perry can level his histogram in several ways. He can change the logic of the schedule so that the number of concurrent activities someone is assigned is less. He can change the relationship between two activities (e.g., change a start-to-start relationship to a finish-to-start one) or add lag between the two activities to reduce concurrency. He can also reduce the float of noncritical activities by lengthening their duration without changing the total hours of effort. Finally, he can reduce the output from certain tasks, thereby leveling the work.

When it becomes impossible to alter the schedule, then Perry can rearrange assignments to lower the working hours per day or employ an

Exhibit 9-2. Leveled histogram.

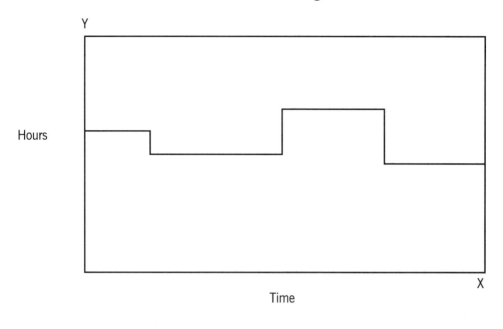

Overtime and Burnout

On many projects, especially ones where meeting the completion date is critical, overtime is the norm rather than the rule. Periodic overtime is fine, but if taken to the extreme, it can have long-term effects on team members and influence overall performance on the project.

From a behavioral perspective, extensive overtime can result in burnout, which is a common condition in the information systems world. Burnout can lead to omissions, rework, and scrapped work, all contributing to lower productivity. From a schedule, cost, and quality perspective, excessive overtime has an effect, too. People's performance becomes impaired.

Too much overtime is symptomatic of major project management problems. There may be an unrealistic schedule, a management-by-crisis situation, poorly trained people, inadequate equipment or facilities, low morale, or lack of teamwork. If excessive overtime becomes the norm, serious replanning is required.

To avoid overtime problems, level the major peaks in the histogram.

Exhibit 9-3. Work assignments.

Task No.	Description	Duration (Days)	Assigned to	Hours/ Day
6.1.1.1	Identify limousine service to church	3	Ewing	8
6.1.1.2	Coordinate limousine service to church	1	Ewing	8
6.1.1.3	Identify limousine service to reception	3	Ewing	8
6.1.1.4	Coordinate limousine service to reception	1	Eisenberg	8
6.1.2.1	Determine transportation requirements to church	3	Ewing	8
6.1.2.2	Coordinate transportation to church	1	Eisenberg	8
6.1.2.3	Determine transportation requirements to and from reception	2	Ewing	8
6.1.2.4	Coordinate transportation to and from reception	1	Eisenberg	8
6.1.2.5	Arrange for valet service for church	1	Smith	8
6.1.2.6	Arrange for valet service for reception	1	Smith	8

alternative person, such as a consultant or contract employee (see "Consultants and Outsources," below).

How Perry Levels the Load

Perry develops a histogram for tasks related to transportation (6.0 in the work breakdown structure). He notices that the histogram for Ewing has high peaks in the beginning and a sharp drop several days later. Exhibit 9-3 shows the assignments of everyone to this task, Exhibit 9-4 shows the original histogram for Ewing, and Exhibit 9-5 shows that portion of the network diagram related to transportation.

Perry figures he has several options:

1. Switch the start-to-start relationship to finish-to-start for tasks 6.1.1.3 or 6.1.2.3, or both with 6.1.1.1.

2. Double the duration but not the work effort (hours) for 6.1.1.2, which is a noncritical-path task.
3. Replace Ewing on certain concurrent tasks (e.g., 6.1.1.1, 6.1.1.3, or 6.1.2.3, or both) with additional help (e.g., consultant, contractor, or outsource). This will reduce the peak for Ewing.
4. Change the precedence relationships between tasks.

After making the changes to the assignments and changing the precedence relationships (see Exhibit 9-6), he generates a leveled histogram for Ewing (see Exhibit 9-7).

CONSULTANTS AND OUTSOURCES

Consultants

From time to time, project managers will not have sufficient labor resources to complete their projects. A solution is to hire consultants.

But hiring consultants should not be done lightly, since their services can prove expensive and the quality of their output is often debatable.

Take the following steps when hiring consultants.

1. Know exactly what you expect from the consultant. Is it a deliverable product? Is it a document or just "advice" in oral form?

2. Look at several consultants rather than one as a sole source. Reliance on one consultant increases dependency.

Exhibit 9-4. Unleveled histogram for Ewing.

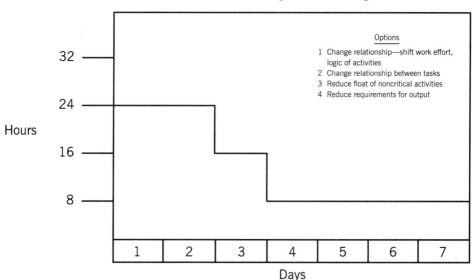

Exhibit 9-5. Network diagram (portion for transportation).

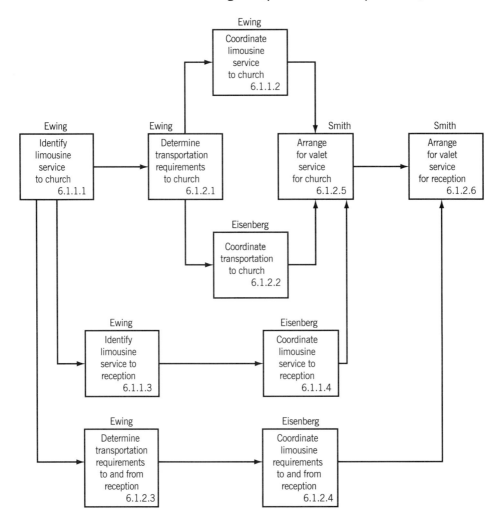

3. Conduct a background investigation. Who is on their client list? How satisfied are the clients with their work? What is their reputability in performing that type of work?

4. Monitor the performance. Expect periodic reviews to preclude the unexpected lack of delivery. Have those reviews documented to prevent legal problems regarding the quality of output.

5. Include the tasks of consultants in the work breakdown structure and on the schedule. If nonperformance occurs, it is easier to show the impact on the overall progress of the project, at least from a schedule and cost perspective.

6. Ensure that the terms and conditions of an agreement exactly describe the deliverable. Don't rely on general statements, which can eventually lead to disagreements that can only be resolved in the courts.

Exhibit 9-6. Network diagram with logic change.

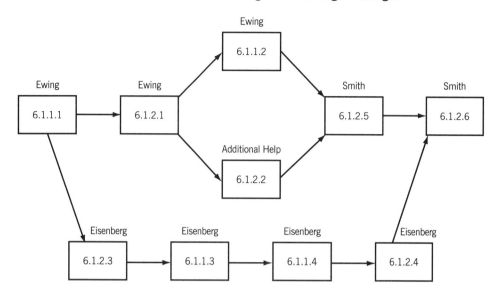

Outsourcing Services

An alternative to using consultants is outsourcing, by which an independent vendor provides a service and assumes responsibility for the results. For example, a project manager might outsource the development and delivery of a deliverable or component of the product being built.

Outsourcing has its advantages. It can help shift the development of difficult, complex deliverables to expertise that does not exist on the team. It can shift nonessential deliverables to outside vendors so that the team can focus on critical matters. Finally, it can allow for flexibility in responding to a fast-paced environment, since less is invested in a project infrastructure and the outsourcing can be canceled without investing too much.

Outsourcing has its disadvantages, too. The potential for losing control may be high. The work can cost more initially. And it takes time to find a reliable outsourcing vendor.

To ensure that you make a good outsourcing decision:

1. Do an analysis to determine if outsourcing is a better option than having the team do the work.
2. Select from several outsourcing vendors. Compare each one, not just on a cost basis but also on reputability of work and service.
3. Identify what is too critical to outsource. A bad outsourcing decision can have disastrous results on the entire project.
4. Identify what you can outsource. Often, these are services or deliverables not essential to the outcome of the project.
5. If outsourcing something critical, then ensure that reviews and

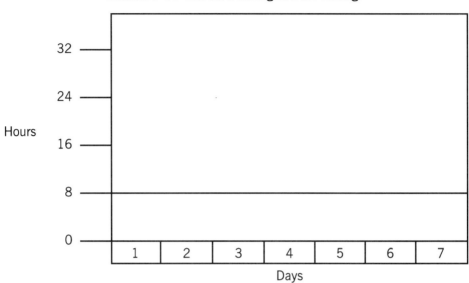

Exhibit 9-7. Leveled histogram for Ewing.

Accelerated Projects

It's called fast-tracking. It is building a product or delivering a service in a very short period of time, usually undertaken for a time-to-market circumstance in an emergency. Information system projects that must deliver an application under market pressure quite commonly fit this category.

People on accelerated projects work at a feverish pace for a short time. There are usually several concurrent activities.

Fast-tracking works best when the project has a previous history, the team members are highly skilled and have previous experience, and the opportunity for reuse exists. The emphasis is on getting results quickly and correctly. Little time is available for experimentation, even creativity.

The downside to fast-tracking is burnout. While the focus on results does provide opportunities for effective teaming, failures can be magnified and lead to finger pointing. Fast-tracking also requires constant training and retraining so people can perform quickly.

Fast-tracking accelerates the life of a project. In exchange for speedy delivery, however, it can have long-term negative consequences.

audits are stipulated in the contract. Actually, the rights for reviews and audits should be incorporated in the contract as a general rule, but especially for critical services or deliverables.

SUMMING UP RESOURCE ALLOCATION

The principles of resource allocation apply to inanimate objects such as desks and supplies no less than to people. In either case allocating resources requires identifying the tasks, making assignments, building profiles, and making adjustments to satisfy requirements. There is, however, one major difference. When doing people allocation, Perry must be sensitive to their psychological needs (e.g., feelings, values), which, of course, is not necessary for inanimate objects. This psychological factor becomes especially important not only when Perry assigns tasks but also when he starts to organize his team to efficiently and effectively achieve the goals of the project.

Questions for Getting Started

1. Did you identify the tasks to allocate your resources?
2. Do you know all the different types of resources you will need?
3. Is there a resource pool where you can get all the resources you need? If not, will you need consultants? Will you need to outsource?
4. Did you assign people to all the tasks?
5. Did you run a resource histogram for each person?
6. Did you need to or attempt to level each of the histograms?
7. When you assign people to tasks, do you consider behavioral as well as technical factors?
8. If you use consultants or outsourcing, did you perform a background analysis first?
9. If overtime appears in the histograms, is it constant or sporadic? If the former, what steps are you willing to take to deal with the effects of burnout?

Chapter 10
Team Organization

Over the years, Perry has seen the symptoms of poor team organization. Some projects have too many leaders, leaving only a few people to do the work and making coordination difficult. Other projects have too many layers of management, impeding effective communication; team members become frustrated, waiting for all the leaders to reach agreement or gain approvals. To augment frustration levels, tasks frequently are unclear, lacking definitions of roles and responsibilities.

Good organization makes sense; yet project managers often give too little attention to organizing their group. Frequently, teams are an assembly of people and nothing more. Some project managers fear alienating people by setting up a project organization. Others lack an appreciation for its contribution to project success. Still others have a preference for an unofficial organizational structure.

Through the function of organization, Perry can realize many advantages. His team can operate more efficiently, since responsibilities and reporting relationships will be clearly defined. It can operate more effectively, because each person will know what is expected of him or her. The team has higher morale, because roles and reporting relationships will be clear—which in turn reduces the opportunities for conflict.

TEN PREREQUISITES FOR EFFECTIVE ORGANIZATION

Perry must satisfy some preliminary requirements to build a formal organization, especially one that handles medium to large projects like his:

1. He must know the project goals. This knowledge will help to determine how to best arrange his resources.
2. He must know all the players. This knowledge will help him to determine who will support him directly and who will provide ad hoc support.
3. He must understand the political climate. Although the team may be temporary, the project may be around for a long time.

4. He must receive preliminary concurrence on the project organization from all the major players (e.g., senior management, customers).

5. He must determine the appropriate span of control. This means determining how many people he can effectively manage before establishing an additional layer of management (e.g., appointing team leaders).

6. He must publish the organization chart as early as possible. This action will clarify roles early and reduce the opportunity for conflict. It will also make assigning responsibilities easier.

7. He must consider how much autonomy to grant people on the project. This will depend on how much control he wants to maintain. If he wants tight control, he will limit the autonomy he grants to project participants.

8. He must consider issues of authority, responsibility, and accountability. How much authority will he have and how much can he grant? How much responsibility can he relinquish and still be accountable for the results?

9. He must consider how to group the functions of the project team. Should he mix them or segregate them? If the latter, how will he encourage information sharing, communication, and teaming?

10. He must identify the line and staff functions. The goal of the project will help determine the positions. Line functions contribute directly to the results; these are typically people on the core team. Staff functions do not contribute directly to the results and ordinarily they are not part of the core team.

TYPES OF ORGANIZATIONAL STRUCTURE

There are two basic types of organizational structures for a project: task force and matrix. The *task force* structure is shown in Exhibit 10-1.

The task force is a group of people assembled to complete a specific goal. The team is completely focused on that goal and, consequently, devotes its entire energies to its accomplishment. By its very nature, task forces are temporary; the team is disassembled once the goal is accomplished. It also usually operates autonomously, with its own budget and authority.

The task force has the advantage of giving visibility to a project. It isolates team members from organizational myopia and frees them from daily administrivia. It enables creativity and experimentation within the confines of the goal and scope of the project.

Despite these advantages, Perry does not like the task force structure, at least for the Smythe Project. Since a task force would last for only a fixed

Exhibit 10-1. Task force structure.

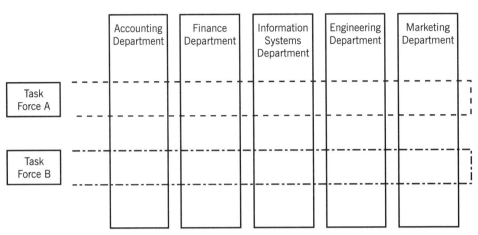

duration, there's a danger that few people would have loyalty to the project and stay the course. As the project experiences difficulties, some people might depart early, leaving it vulnerable to schedule slippages and lapses in quality.

As the project grows, too, it can become too independent, "stealing" people from other projects. Other organizations and projects are robbed of badly needed expertise. As a project ends, the task force may experience severe morale problems, as people scramble for new jobs before completing their responsibilities. It is not uncommon for a project to experience lapses in quality as a result.

Keeping these shortcomings in mind, Perry agrees with his boss that a matrix structure is best for the Smythe Project. A *matrix structure* obtains resources from functional organizations and also shares those people with other projects. For command and control purposes, people report to their functional managers but support one or more project managers. A generic matrix structure is shown in Exhibit 10-2 and the one for the Smythe wedding is shown in Exhibit 10-3.

The matrix structure offers several advantages. It allows for sharing people with heavy expertise among several projects. People don't need to look for a new job as the project concludes. The project manager can acquire people with the right skills at the right time, thereby reducing the need to keep people on when they are not needed; this helps keep the cost lower. The matrix structure also gives senior management flexibility in changing the scope or stopping the project owing to different market conditions.

Perry realizes, though, that a matrix structure presents challenges. It makes planning difficult, especially if projects are sharing resources. Often, he must negotiate with functional and other managers to obtain people's help.

Exhibit 10-2. Matrix structure.

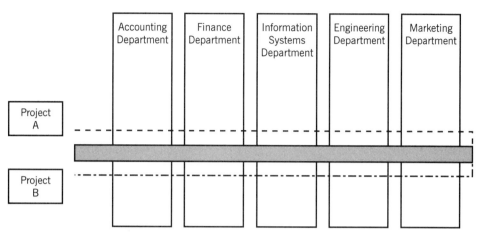

A matrix structure can wreak havoc on morale, too. Team members on multiple projects may be forced to determine which project to give attention to. Sometimes the competition is so keen that individuals become pawns in a power struggle among functional and project managers. That struggle can last a long time, adding to team angst. Finally, the matrix structure often violates the unity-of-command principle (a single superior to whom subordinates report).

To tackle these challenges, Perry recognizes the stress a matrix structure places on team members. He will coordinate closely with functional and other project managers to facilitate availability and try to integrate his project with other projects. He will encourage greater communication, information sharing, and bonding. Finally, he will stress flexibility; change is a way of life in the matrix environment, since priorities and resource availabilities constantly change.

VIRTUAL TEAMS

Recent advances in information systems have brought unparalleled changes to business, not just technically but also in managing projects. These changes include e-mail, the Internet, groupware, and client-server technology. Technologies such as these have enabled team members to work autonomously at remote locations during all time periods (e.g., mornings, evenings). But a project team may never meet face-to-face with some people and will only interact electronically. That is the nature of virtual teams.

There are many advantages to a virtual team. It reduces the need for expensive facilities. Team members feel greater freedom, working with less supervision. A side benefit is a flatter organization chart, too.

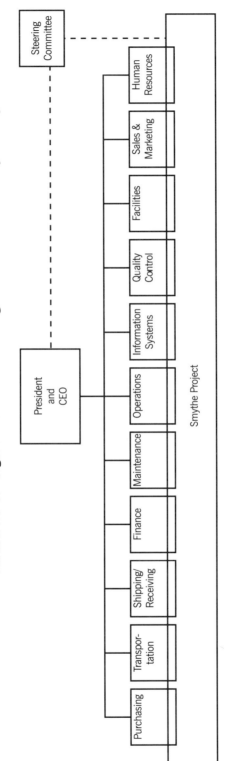

Exhibit 10-3. Organization chart reflecting matrix structure of Smythe Project.

While sounding like a dream come true, reality may provide a different picture. Virtual teams can pose tough challenges. The first is how to provide support for these virtual team members. There are issues concerning hardware and software, plus administrative matters such as accessibility to the project library and ways of collecting information nonelectronically.

Second is how to overcome the purported loneliness that affects some virtual team members. Many work alone, in remote geographical locations. Their opportunities for social interaction and camaraderie are limited.

Third is the challenge of coordinating the activities of team members. With members geographically dispersed and in different time zones, coordination can be a nightmare. Since oversight is difficult, project managers cannot closely monitor work. Similarly, communication usually involves more than e-mail. There must be a way to discuss major project activities.

Some ways to handle these challenges include:

- Conducting frequent face-to-face meetings and holding social gatherings
- Developing objective ways to measure performance and completion criteria
- Empowering people to assume responsibility and accountability for results
- Establishing time commitments for team members to respond to each other
- Providing a standard suite of hardware and software tools

SWAT Teams

Special Weapons and Tactics (SWAT) teams are a growing presence in project management. These are small groups of individuals who are experts not just in project management but also in other subjects. In the sense that their objective is to move quickly to complete their mission and pull out, these groups are like the police SWAT teams from which they get their name. Specifically, a project SWAT team must quickly set up the appropriate project management and technical disciplines at the beginning of a project. Once the disciplines have been established, the team relinquishes control to a project manager and his group, who are responsible for completing the project.

SWAT team work is intense. By the time its work is completed, it will have developed and implemented a complete project plan, from estimates to schedules.

Although hard skills (e.g., expertise with software and hardware) are important, soft skills are important, too. For example, SWAT team members must solicit buy-in for their work. Active listening, facilitation, communication, and teaming skills are extremely important. Also important is the ability to keep calm under pressure and a willingness to share equipment, expertise, or information.

To use SWAT teams effectively:

1. Obtain support for the work of a SWAT team by follow-on teleconferencing sessions; otherwise, the team's effort will be wasted.
2. Be aware that working on a SWAT team can cause burnout. Morale and energy levels can plummet.
3. Provide constant training for SWAT team members. They must keep abreast of technologies in order to provide state-of-the-art expertise. Cross-training can help, but only so far.
4. Select people for the SWAT team who can handle ambiguity. Members must be willing to tackle projects when goals and deliverables are ill defined.

SELF-DIRECTED WORK TEAMS

In recent years, a different approach to building teams has emerged, called a Self-Directed Work Team (SDWT).

SDWTs are teams that have considerable autonomy while building a product or delivering a service. It is a group of professionals sharing responsibility for results.

These teams are cross-functional, meaning that people with different disciplines and backgrounds work together to achieve a common goal. The team decides everything, from setting priorities to allocating resources. Other actions include selecting people, evaluating performance, and improving processes. The key characteristic is the autonomy to make decisions without supervisory approval.

Several trends are pushing toward the SDWT concept because these teams:

- Create flatter organizations
- Empower employees
- Encourage greater teaming
- Encourage people to have a more general background
- Enlarge spans of control

SDWTs are excellent candidates for applying project management ideas. Since the entire team is responsible for the results, all members must help lead, define, plan, organize, control, and close the project. The tools and techniques of project management enable teams to do that.

Questions for Getting Started

1. Did you determine whether your project organization has or should have a task force or matrix structure?
2. Regardless of the type, did you consider the following when organizing the team:
   - Accountability issues?
   - Authority issues?
   - Basis for grouping functions?
   - Concurrence from the right people?
   - Level of autonomy for team members?
   - Players?
   - Political climate?
   - Project goals?
   - Responsibility issues?
   - Span of control?
   - When to publish the organization chart?
   - Which are the line and which are the staff functions?
3. If a task force structure, what can you do to deal with its shortcomings (e.g., decline in loyalty)?
4. If a matrix structure, what can you do to deal with its shortcomings (e.g., competition among projects for key people)?
5. If you have a virtual team, even partially, how will you deal with the challenges (e.g., ongoing technical support) often associated with such teams?
6. If you have a SWAT team, how will you overcome the challenges (e.g., burnout) often associated with such teams?

Chapter 11

Budget Development and Cost Calculation

Nothing gets done without money. Projects are no exception, and Perry is the first to realize this.

There are many reasons for calculating costs before they are incurred. To begin, they give an idea of how much the goals will cost to achieve. Cost calculations later become a tool for measuring the efficiency of a project team. They also help determine priorities as the project progresses. Finally, they contribute to the overall profitability of a company.

As project manager, Perry has several responsibilities for budgeting. He must develop budgets on a task-by-task basis and for the entire project. He must ensure that expenditures stay within the budget allocated for each task and the project as a whole. He seeks additional funding, if necessary. Finally, he tracks and monitors expenditures, identifying and reporting deviations to upper management.

When estimating his costs, Perry establishes a *management reserve,* usually 3 to 5 percent of the total estimate for the project, to address unexpected costs. This reserve increases the overall cost estimate for the project.

Later, while controlling his project, Perry uses the cost estimates to compare to actual expenditures. Of particular importance are estimates versus actual costs up to a given point. If the actual costs exceed the estimated costs up to a specific point, an overrun exists. If the actual costs are less than the estimated costs up to a specific point, an underrun exists. Perry looks for overruns and underruns on a task-by-task global basis. If the feedback has an overrun, for example, Perry takes corrective action.

DIFFERENT KINDS OF COSTS

Perry knows that many items in a project cost money. The typical ones are:

- Equipment (purchase, lease, rental, and usage)
- Facilities (office space, warehouses)

- Labor (employee, contract)
- Supplies (paper, pencils, toner, sundries)
- Training (seminars, conferences, symposiums)
- Transportation (land, sea, air)

The standard formulas for calculating these costs are:

$$\text{Equipment} = \text{purchase price}$$
or
$$\text{lease price} \times \text{time period}$$
or
$$\text{rental price} \times \text{time period}$$

$$\text{Facilities} = \text{lease price} \times \text{time period}$$
or
$$\text{rental price} \times \text{time period}$$

$$\text{Labor costs} = (\text{regular hours} \times \text{hourly rate}) + (\text{overtime hours} \times \text{time and a half rate}) + (\text{overtime hours} \times \text{double time rate})$$

$$\text{Supplies} = \text{quantity} \times \text{unit price}$$

$$\text{Training costs} = (\text{tuition cost} \times \text{number of attendees}) + (\text{the sum of the labor costs for attendees})$$

$$\text{Transportation costs} = (\text{daily, weekly, monthly, or hourly rate}) \times (\text{period of usage})$$

There are also different ways to classify costs.

Direct vs. Indirect Costs

Direct costs directly relate to the building of a product—for example, materials and specialized labor. Indirect costs are other than direct costs and not necessarily related to the building of a product—for example, rent and taxes.

Recurring vs. Nonrecurring Costs

Recurring costs appear regularly—for example, long-term payments for facilities. Nonrecurring costs appear only once—for example, the purchase of equipment.

Fixed vs. Variable Costs

Fixed costs are not alterable owing to changes in work volume—for example, cost of facilities usage. Variable costs vary depending upon consumption and workload—for example, cost of materials.

Activity-Based Costing (ABC)

Activity-based costing (ABC) is a process approach to accounting, giving a realistic portrait of the total costs for a project. With traditional accounting methods, labor is seen as the primary contributor to costs, while with ABC, overhead and materials have significant impact. Traditional accounting emphasizes "hacking away many heads," not reducing material and overhead costs. ABC instead focuses on processes and their improvement, not just reducing head count. It also focuses on customers, since the true cost of the final product is passed on to the customers.

Project managers can play a major role in furthering the use of ABC. ABC also requires good definitions of what the customer wants (statement of work), a list of the activities for meeting those wants (work breakdown structure), and fixed monies (cost estimates) to produce the product or deliver the service. Project managers can realistically determine direct and indirect costs and also determine what processes to improve or remove in order to increase customer satisfaction and reduce costs.

Burdened vs. Nonburdened Labor Rates

Burdened labor rates include the cost of fringe benefits—for example, insurance and floor space and nonlabor overhead. Nonburdened rates are labor rates minus the cost of fringe benefits and overhead.

Regular vs. Overtime Labor Rates

Regular labor rates are less than or equal to 40 hours per week. Overtime labor rates are more than 40 hours per week, including time and a half and overtime.

HOW TO CALCULATE COSTS

Making a reliable cost estimate depends on the amount of information available for estimating. Having more information means you have greater ability to discern the elements that constitute an estimate. Making a reliable cost estimate also depends on a good work breakdown structure (WBS); see Chapter 6. And, of course, to produce a reliable cost estimate requires a good project definition; the better the definition, the more reliable the estimate because the parameters of the final product or service have been established; see Chapter 5.

Obtaining a reliable cost estimate depends on good time estimates, too. Most cost estimates rely on a count of labor hours to complete work. If the work estimate is reliable, then the costs should have an equivalent reliability, since they represent hourly rate times total hours; see Chapter 7. Finally, estimates often are based on assumptions. Unless identified, these assumptions can lead to misunderstandings and ultimately to inaccurate calculations. The assumptions are spelled out in the statement of work; see Chapter 5.

What follows is an example of how Perry estimates the costs for each task in the WBS. He uses a worksheet format (Exhibit 11-1) to calculate the figures. The summary of his calculations is the total cost for the project, excluding the management reserve.

Perry tracks the estimate-at-completion for each task and the management-estimate-at-completion (MEAC). The estimate-at-completion is a combination of actual expenditures to date up to a specific point plus the remaining estimate to complete the project. The MEAC is the actual expenditures to date plus the remaining estimate to complete the entire project. Both the estimate-at-completion and the actual expenditures to date give

Exhibit 11-1. Worksheet for estimating costs.

Task 6.1.2.2: Coordinate Transportation to Church.

Assignment	Regular Hours	Rate ($ per)	Time and a Half Hours	Rate ($ per)	Double Time Hours	Rate ($ per)
Eisenberg	16	35.00	—		—	

	Costs ($)
Labor	560.00
Telephone	12.00
Transportation	20.00
Training	0.00
Equipment	0.00
Supplies	0.00
Total Estimate	592.00 round to 600.00

Perry a good idea of how well expenditures have gone and will go if the current levels of performance continue.

WHAT HAPPENS IF COST ESTIMATES ARE TOO HIGH?

Frequently, project managers are asked to reduce their estimates. Top management often feels that a project can be completed with less money. It may even declare a 10 percent across-the-board reduction for all projects. Dealing with such commands is one of the hardest challenges facing project managers. Fortunately, they have several options.

The project manager can communicate her reasons for the cost estimates. She can explain, for example, the rationale behind the time estimates and the accompanying calculations. Presenting the reasons and assumptions especially gives a persuasive argument for retaining the cost estimates.

The project manager can also develop revised cost estimates. Based on feedback from senior management, she can select the best revised estimate.

Finally, the project manager can negotiate with the customer to reduce or revise the scope of the project, reduce the work requirements as described in the work breakdown structure, reduce the time estimates, and modify the assignments. Ultimately, revisions to the scope will then be reflected in the estimated costs.

THE KEY: IDENTIFYING AND MANAGING COSTS

Money is the oil that gets projects moving and keeps them running. The Smythe Project is no exception. Perry appreciates the importance of identifying and managing costs throughout the life of the project. He knows that how he categorizes costs is not as important as ensuring that the project completes within budget.

Perry knows, too, that costs, along with schedules, are susceptible to positive and negative changes that may increase or decrease the reliability of his estimates. To a large extent, this reliability will be affected by the degree of risk associated with his schedule and cost estimates.

Questions for Getting Started

1. Did you identify all the types of costs for your project?
2. Did you identify the rates for usage and quantity that you plan to consume?

3. Did you calculate the total costs by summing the totals for each task?
4. If you elect to have a management reserve, did you determine the appropriate percent to be multiplied against the total costs of the tasks?
5. If you received pressure from your management or the customer for having too high an estimate, did you develop alternative ways to deal with their resistance?

Chapter 12

Risk Management

Projects can fail for a number of reasons and the risks are always high. While a project manager cannot eliminate risk, she can prevent or mitigate its impacts by using risk management.

MANAGING RISK: A FOUR-STEP PROCESS

Risk management is the process of identifying, analyzing, controlling, and reporting risk. Risk *identification* is the identification of major elements of a project and their associated risks. To do this, Perry will rely on his and others' knowledge and expertise. He will meet with core team members, the customer, and senior management to solicit input. He will review documentation, including the statement of work, work breakdown structure, and requirements documents. This information prepares him for the next step. Risk *analysis* is the classification of those elements to different levels of risk. Perry will compare the "should be" controls with the ones that do exist and will identify any discrepancies. He will also determine the probability or likelihood each risk will materialize and whether a control is necessary. Risk *control* is the determination of controls that can mitigate the risks. It involves deciding under what circumstances to take action to prevent or mitigate the impact of a risk. Perry essentially will do contingency planning, which involves anticipating responses to negative circumstances. Risk *reporting* is the act of informing team members and senior management of those risks.

Perry knows that by managing risk, he can identify priorities, thereby focusing his energies and resources as well as developing a meaningful project plan. The analysis of risk indicates the strengths and the weaknesses of the project, so that he can maximize his assets and minimize his losses. It helps him to identify and put into place the most important controls, rather try to control everything.

To perform risk management, Perry needs information, time, expertise, and perspective. The information is necessary to understand the major processes and components, the accompanying threats, and the controls that should be in place. It will take time to collect the information and assemble it in some meaningful form. He will use his expertise in project management to apply risk management while maintaining a broad perspective to avoid focusing on just one area (e.g., technical issues at the expense of business ones).

EXPOSURE

Several factors can expose projects to higher than normal risk.

- **Team size.** The larger the team, the higher the probability of a problem arising. For example, communications can be more difficult as the number of participants increases. The number of interactions among people increases and thus they require greater coordination.

- **History.** Newer projects are riskier because the processes have not been refined. The more times a project of a similar nature has been done, the greater the likelihood of success.

- **Staff expertise and experience.** If the staff lacks direct experience and knowledge of the subject, people will struggle to learn as they go along, robbing the project of time and possibly introducing errors.

- **Complexity.** The more sophisticated a project, the greater the opportunity of a mistake or slipup. Untested technologies, such as ones dealing with information systems or biotechnologies, are risk laden.

- **Management stability.** The more senior management plays "musical chairs," the greater the risks of a problem arising. With every new management comes the possibility of changed priorities and directions. Management stability implies unity of direction, which in turn means reaching goals. Management irritability can lead to unrealistic scheduling and inefficient use of resources.

- **Time compression.** If a schedule is highly compressed, then the risks are magnified. Having more time means greater flexibility and the opportunity to prevent or mitigate the impact of errors.

- **Resource availability.** The more resources that are available, the greater the ability to respond to problems as they arise. For example, more money brings greater ability to secure equipment or people when needed. Plentiful resources, of course, do not guarantee protection from risk; however they do provide the means to respond to it.

CATEGORIES OF RISK

Risks can be viewed as business, technical, or operational. An example of a business risk is misuse of project funds. A technical risk is the inability to build the product that will satisfy requirements. An operational risk is the inability of the customer to work with core team members.

Risks are either acceptable or unacceptable. An acceptable risk is one that negatively affects a task on the noncritical path. An unacceptable risk is one that negatively affects the critical path.

Risks are either short or long term. A short-term risk has an immediate impact, such as changing the requirements for a deliverable. A long-term risk has an impact sometime in the distant future, such as releasing a product without adequate testing.

Risks are viewed as either manageable or unmanageable. A manageable risk is one you can live with, such as a minor requirement change. An unmanageable risk is impossible to accommodate, such as a huge turnover of core team members.

Finally, risks are either internal or external. An internal risk is peculiar to a project, such as the inability to get the parts of a product to work. An external risk originates from outside the scope of the project, such as when senior management arbitrarily cuts funding by 20 percent.

Categorizing risks is, of course, mainly an academic exercise. These classifications can help you determine the source, relative importance, and impact to the project.

KEY CONCEPTS IN RISK MANAGEMENT

When performing risk management, Perry remembers the following concepts.

■ A *component* is a basic element of an overall system. A project is a system consisting of components that, in turn, can consist of subcomponents. Components can be processes, deliverables, or both. Examples of a component are a process like "determining requirements" or a deliverable like a "requirements document."

■ A *threat* is the occurrence of an event that negatively affects a project in some manner. A threat exploits a vulnerability, or exposure. An example of a threat is when there is no customer buy-in of a schedule or requirement. A *vulnerability* is the inherent degree of weakness of a component, such as a schedule having no acceptance by the customer.

■ *Probability* is the odds that something, like a threat, will occur anywhere from 0 to 100 percent. Probability determines the extent to which a risk will occur and the level of vulnerability.

- *Control* is a measure in place to mitigate, prevent, or correct the impact of a threat. A control can be physical, such as a required signature, or logical, such as a peer review.

Keeping the above concepts in mind, Perry can perform risk management using two approaches: quantitative or qualitative.

The *quantitative approach* relies on statistical calculation to determine risk, its probability of occurrence, and its impact on a project. A common example of the quantitative approach is decision tree analysis, applying probabilities to two or more outcomes. Another example is the three-point estimating technique described in Chapter 7. Still another approach is the Monte Carlo simulation, which generates a value from a probability distribution and other factors.

The *qualitative approach* relies on judgments, using criteria to determine outcomes. A common qualitative approach is a precedence diagramming method, which uses ordinal numbers to determine priorities and outcomes. Another approach is heuristics, or rules of thumb, to determine outcomes.

An example of a qualitative approach is to list in descending order specific processes of a project, the risk or risks associated with each process, and the control or controls that may or should exist for each risk. See Exhibit 12-1.

WAYS TO HANDLE RISK

There are four basic ways to deal with risk.

1. Accept the risk, known as *risk acceptance*. Perry can do nothing to prevent or mitigate the impact of a risk. For example, he continues to

Exhibit 12-1. Example of a qualitative approach.

Process	Risk	Control
1. Obtain involvement of client.	Inability to make regular contact.	Mail or e-mail duplicate copies of project management documentation to the client.
2. Determine requirements.	Unclear requirements.	Conduct periodic reviews.
	Unavailable requirements.	Draft requirements and review them with client.

address the same requirements despite management having reduced the budget.

2. Adapt to the risk, known as *risk adaptation*. Perry can take measures that will mitigate the impact of a risk. For example, he reduces requirements to reflect the corresponding cutback in funding.

3. Avoid the risk, known as *risk avoidance*. Perry takes action that will keep a risk from seriously impacting his project. For example, he decides to narrow the scope of the project to avoid certain high risks.

4. Transfer the risk, known as *risk transfer*. Perry lets someone else assume the risk. For example, he contracts out or outsources certain high-risk tasks rather than let the core team handle them.

When performing the contingency planning, Perry will identify the expected event or threat, its probability of occurrence, and its impacts (e.g., economic, technical, operational), and then devise an appropriate response. He uses a simple form to capture this information, as shown in Exhibit 12-2.

Perry also reviews the schedule to identify possible risks. He considers options like changing the dependencies, durations, requirements, resource assignments, or time estimates.

RISK REPORTING

Risk reporting occurs after risk identification, analysis, and control are complete. Perry has the option to develop either a written or an oral report. In either case, however, the content of the report will be basically the same.

A risk report should be clear, concise, and self-explanatory. It should contain categories of risks (e.g., business and technical); components; risks for each component, to include probability of occurrence and impact; background and scope of project; and recommendations or actions to strengthen controls or respond to risks when they become actual problems (e.g., contingency plans).

Exhibit 12-2. Risk response form.

Description	Probability of Occurrence	Impacts	Response
Cancellation of air transportation	Low	▪ Less attendance at reception or wedding ▪ Delays in arrivals	Set up charter flight

THE KEY: RISK MANAGEMENT, NOT ELIMINATION

In a dynamic environment, a project will always face risks. The key is not to try to eliminate risks but to manage them. Perry identifies and analyzes risks. He then implements controls to mitigate or eliminate their potential impact. However, he also communicates the list of risks and their accompanying controls to all people who have a need to know. By developing and distributing documentation on risks and their controls, Perry can either prevent related problems or minimize their effects when they occur.

Questions for Getting Started

1. Did you identify the major components and processes for your project?
2. Did you identify the major threats to your project? Did you identify their probability of occurrence?
3. Did you identify the controls that should exist for preventing or mitigating risks to each component or process?
4. Did you conduct research to determine what controls actually exist?
5. For all control weaknesses, did you determine whether contingency plans should be in place? If so, did you prepare the appropriate response?

Chapter 13

Project Documentation: Procedures, Forms, Memos, and Such

Perry recognizes that documentation is essential for leading, defining, planning, organizing, controlling, and closing a project. He also realizes that too much documentation is as much a problem as too little. A balance must exist, depending largely on the size and importance of the project.

Good documentation serves as an excellent communication tool. It provides an audit trail for analysis and project reviews. It lends order and structure to the project by giving direction and setting parameters. It increases efficiency and effectiveness because everyone follows the "same sheet of music." And it gives team members confidence, especially when things appear chaotic or there are too many unknowns.

Project documentation consists of the following items:

- Procedures
- Flowcharts
- Forms
- Reports
- Memos
- Project manual
- Project library
- Newsletters
- History files

PROCEDURES

For many projects, particularly large ones, procedures facilitate management. They help achieve efficiency by ensuring consistency of action. They improve effectiveness by ensuring that people achieve project goals. They

Key Insights for Preparing Procedures

Developing procedures is more than just writing words on paper. Regardless of your writing ability, consider the following when developing procedures.

1. Define acronyms the first time they appear and spell out abbreviations at first use. The reader may not know what you mean.
2. Define special terms. The reader needs to understand what you are saying.
3. Avoid clichés. They are a tired way of expressing what you mean. Be original—but always clear in your meaning.
4. Check for typographical and spelling errors. They distract from the message and show sloppiness.
5. Use positive expressions. Avoid "do not" or "cannot" because such phrases create a mental block in the reader's mind. Be positive.
6. Use the active rather than the passive voice. The active voice is strong language; the passive voice is weak and reveals a tentative writer.
7. Watch your organization. Ideas should flow logically, such as from the general to the specific, or vice versa. Chronological order is also good.
8. Avoid wordiness. Keep sentences short (less than 15 words) and paragraphs brief (usually less than 5 sentences). Ideas are easier to grasp this way.
9. Integrate text and graphics. If using both, ensure that the text references the graphics and that the two match information.
10. Track your revisions. Assign a version number to each and note the date, so everyone uses the most recent version.

reduce the learning curve by providing guidance on the "way things are done." Finally, they improve productivity because people with questions can refer to the documentation rather than interrupt other people.

To develop a good set of procedures, you need the following:

- Information to write about the topic
- Time to prepare, review, and publish the documents

- People with good research, writing, and editing skills
- Management and user buy-in to ensure people follow the proce-
dures
- Feedback loop to ensure completeness, currency, and usability

Procedures are often less than adequate on projects, for several reasons. For one, the project manager may view writing procedures as something that must be done only to "satisfy requirements." The results are
poorly written and incomplete procedures. Or the project manager may
assign the task to someone who knows little about the project or whose
role is minimal. Sometimes the project manager prepares the procedures
late in the project, mainly to satisfy reviewers and auditors. Finally, the
procedures are prepared and then set on a shelf, never to be used by
anyone.

Perry, of course, ensures good procedures by following four simple
steps.

1. **Identify the topics.** Perry can either develop a set of topics on his
own or solicit help from the team. He chooses the latter, as well as con-
ducts research on previous projects to find similar procedures.

Some specific topics include:

- Change control
- Forms
- Meetings
- Organizational structure
- Purchases
- Reports
- Resource usage
- Responsibilities
- Schedules
- Statusing

2. **Determine the format for the procedures.** There are four possible
procedure formats: narrative (Exhibit 13-1), sequential (Exhibit 13-2), playscript (Exhibit 13-3), and item-by-item (Exhibit 13-4). As Exhibit 13-1 demon-
strates, the narrative format has an essaylike appearance. Although a narrative
presentation is easy to read, information within it is often hard to find quickly.
Also, it causes eyestrain, since the blocks of text minimize white space. And it
is difficult to update or revise because it lacks modularity.

The sequential format, as shown in Exhibit 13-2, has a step-by-step
appearance. Each sentence is a generally brief command. Its brevity, abundant white space, and simplicity make it easy to follow and find information. It is best used for procedures involving one person.

Exhibit 13-1. Narrative format.

Completing and Submitting the Monthly Status Report Form

Project: _____

Date: _____

Start (baseline): _____

Finish (baseline): _____

Management estimate at
  completion (MEAC) date: _____

Variance: _____

Original total cost estimate: _____

Estimated cost to date: _____

Actual cost to date: _____

Management estimate at
  completion (MEAC) cost: _____

Variance: _____

Overall performance evaluation: _____

This procedure describes how to complete and submit the Monthly Status Report (MSR) form, which is shown above.

The MSR must be completed to track and monitor the performance of your project. It is therefore important to complete all fields and submit the form on time.

In the project field, write the name of the project. Be sure to add the project number if one has been assigned. In the date field, write the date you are completing the form, using the month/day/year format (e.g., 11/26/00). In the start (baseline) field, write the original start date using the same format as the one for the date field. Do the same for the finish (baseline) field. In the management estimate at completion (MEAC) date field, record the actual progress to date plus the remaining estimate of the work to be completed. In the variance field, write the difference in days between the MEAC and the original finish date. In the total cost estimate field, write the original estimated cost for the project. . . .[1]

After completing the MSR, make three copies. Keep one copy for your records. Submit one copy to your next higher level of management or to the chairman of your steering committee, if applicable. Then attach the remaining copy to the original and submit both to the Project Review Office (PRO) at mail stop 78H1.

One final note. The PRO must have possession of the MSR no later than the final working day of a month.

1. *Authors' note:* This example of the narrative format would actually have been one paragraph longer; however, we deleted the instructions for the last five fields to spare our readers.

Exhibit 13-2. Sequential format.

Monthly Status Report Form

Instructions: Complete each field according to the procedure Completing the Monthly Status Report Form, below. Make a copy for your records and forward the original to the Program Office, mailstop 3X-41.

Project: **A**   Date: **B**

Schedule:
    Start Baseline: **C**
    Finish Baseline: **D**
    Management Estimate at Completion Date: **E**
    Variance: **F**

Budget:
    Original Total Cost Estimate: **G**
    Estimated Cost to Date: **H**
    Actual Cost to Date: **I**
    Management Estimate at Completion: **J**
    Variance: **K**

Overall Performance Evaluation: **L**

⸙

Completing the Monthly Status Report Form

This procedure describes how to complete the Monthly Status Report form.

1. Obtain a copy of the form from the project office.

2. Answer each field on the form by matching the applicable letter below with the corresponding one shown in the figure on the next page.

    A. Name of the project
    B. Date you completed the form
    C. The original start date in month/day/year format
    D. The original finish date in month/day/year format
    E. The date reflecting actual progress-to-date plus the remaining estimate of the work to be completed in month/day/year format
    F. The difference in days between the management estimate at completion and the original finish date
    G. The original estimated cost for the project
    H. The original estimated cost up to a specific date
    I. The costs accrued up to a specific date
    J. The actual costs accrued up to a specific date plus the remaining estimated costs to complete the project
    K. The original total estimated cost minus management at completion cost
    L. Your opinion about the overall progress of the project as well as a description of the major cost, budget, requirements, and technical issues impacting the project

Exhibit 13-3. Playscript format.

Processing the Monthly Status Report Form

The procedure describes how to process the Monthly Status Report Form. It does not explain how to complete it. For that, refer to the procedure Completing the Monthly Status Report Form.

PROJECT MANAGER
1. Obtain a copy of the Monthly Status Report Form.
2. Complete the Monthly Status Report Form.
3. Date and sign the form.
4. Make two (2) photocopies.
    a. Retain one copy for the project history file.
    b. Attach the other copy to the master document.

PROGRAM OFFICE
1. Review the Monthly Status Report Form for completeness.
2. If incomplete:
    a. Prepare a memo noting the shortcomings.
    b. Attach a copy of the memo to the master document.
    c. File the copy.
    d. Return the memo and master copy to the project manager.

3. If complete:
    a. Date-stamp the master document and photocopy.
    b. File the master copy.
    c. Return the copy to the project manager.

As with the sequential format, the playscript format (Exhibit 13-3) has a step-by-step appearance and possesses the same structure. Similarly, its brief style, abundant white space, and simplicity make it easy to follow and to find information. It is best used for procedures involving two or more people.

The item-by-item format, shown in Exhibit 13-4, has all the characteristics and advantages of the sequential and playscript formats. It works best, however, when a procedure covers a mixture of topics.

3. **Prepare, review, revise, and publish the procedure.** This step should involve as much participation as possible by members of the team, so as to seek buy-in from those who must follow the procedures. Here is an outline of a typical procedure:

    I. Purpose
   II. Scope
  III. Contents

Exhibit 13-4. Item-by-item format.

Handling All Reports for Competitive-Sensitive Projects

This procedure describes how to handle reports generated for projects designated proprietary.

I. Cost Report
    A. Review the report.
    B. Store one copy of the report in a secure room, drawer, or safe.
    C. Shred any additional copies.

II. Schedule Report
    A. Review the report.
    B. Store one copy of the report in a secure room, drawer, or safe.
    C. Shred any additional copies.

III. Monthly Status Report
    A. Complete the report.
    B. Upon receiving the date-stamped copy from the program office, shred the original.
    C. Store the retained copy in a secure room, drawer, or safe.

    IV. Approvals
     V. Appendices

4. **Follow the procedures.** At first the comment might sound academic; however, many projects have written procedures, let alone plans, that no one follows. In the end, the procedures serve no function other than to occupy a bare spot on a shelf.

FLOWCHARTS

Many times, pictures and diagrams are preferred over text or are treated as supplements to text. Flowcharts indeed are worth a thousand words.

Flowcharts are easier to understand than written procedures and communicate more with less. However, even using flowcharts requires effort. It takes time to prepare them. They must be updated to maintain relevancy. And users and management must buy in to them if the project manager expects people to follow them.

When developing flowcharts, keep the following points in mind.

1. Use symbols consistently. Provide a key to the symbols.
2. Put the flowcharts under version control. Different versions can quickly be released, thereby confusing people.

3. Use a software tool to generate the diagrams. Revisions will be easier and the charts clearer.
4. Keep it simple. Avoid putting too much on a page. A cluttered page can be as mentally taxing as large blocks of small text on a page.

There are a number of flowcharting techniques. Some charts show the flow of control (e.g., do step 1, then step 2, and, if positive, do step 3). Others show the flow of data (e.g., the use of early and late dates and durations to calculate float). Exhibits 13-5 and 13-6 have flowcharts showing flow of control and data flow, respectively.

When flowcharting, follow these four steps:

1. Determine the topic, just as you would with written procedures.
2. Determine the type of diagram and whether it is a substitute or a complement to a procedure. Flow of control is the most popular, followed by data flow diagrams.
3. Prepare, review, revise, and publish the flowchart. This step is the same for procedures.
4. Follow the flowchart. Like procedures, they can quickly end up covering a bare spot on a bookshelf.

FORMS

Although many people dislike completing forms, Perry sees their value in managing his project. Forms capture and communicate information. They also provide audit trails to help learn from past experience, compile statistics, and conduct postimplementation reviews.

Unfortunately, many forms are not user-friendly. The instructions for completion and distribution are unclear. The fields do not flow logically. They ask for way too much information. And there are usually too many forms of too many varieties.

Ideally, forms should have these qualities:

- Be logically organized
- Be readily available
- Not exceed one page
- List a source and destination
- Have clear and concise instructions for completion and submission
- Have adequate space for filling in information
- Request only the necessary information

For use in project management, forms can capture information on such topics as activity descriptions, Activity estimating, assignments,

Exhibit 13-5. Flow of control.

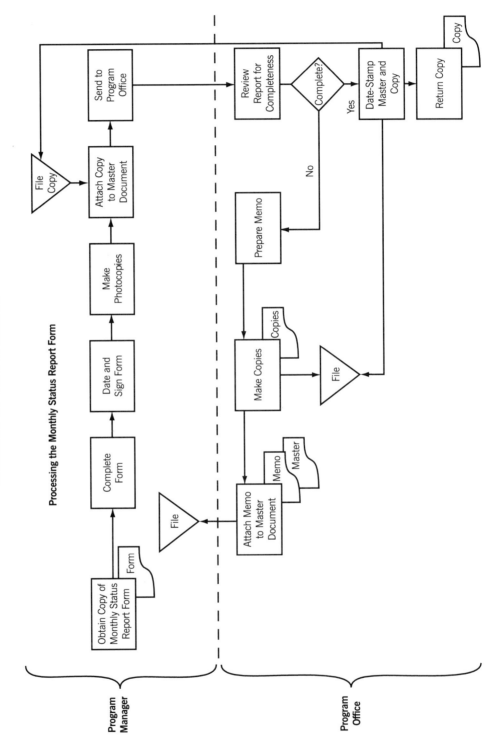

Processing the Monthly Status Report Form

Exhibit 13-6. Data flow.

Processing the Monthly Status Report Form

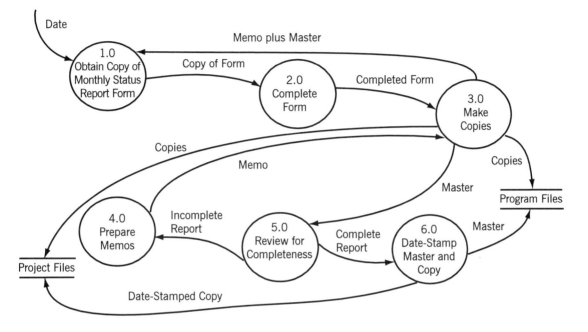

change management, estimated labor usage, labor and nonlabor costs, problem identification and tracking, and status of activities.

Here are some guidelines on how to prepare a usable form:

1. Determine its purpose (e.g., capturing schedule or cost data).
2. Determine who will complete the form and who will process it.
3. Identify the exact data to capture.
4. Determine its source and destination.
5. Prepare the instructions for its completion.
6. Prepare a draft of the form (e.g., using a graphics or spreadsheet program).
7. Circulate the form for evaluation (e.g., to people who can complete it and to others who will use data that it captures).
8. Make revisions, if necessary.
9. Determine the number of copies and how the copies will be made.
10. Reproduce the form.
11. Distribute it either electronically or in hard copy.

Exhibit 13-7 is an example of a well-defined form.

Perry performs four steps to draw up forms for his project.

Distribution Methods

There are essentially two ways to present forms, reports, memos, and the like.

- **Hard copy.** Traditional papers, usually typed or printed. It has the advantage of being familiar; the downside is that it can be costly to maintain, labor-intensive to revise, difficult to keep current, highly prone to human error, and takes up file space.
- **Electronic copy.** On computer disk or tape. Electronic copies can reduce the need for storage space, lower labor-intensive actions (e.g., revisions), and make updating easier. Unfortunately, electronic copies still remain susceptible to human error, although less so with the recent advances in electronic storage. Hard copy backups have been the norm, here.

Electronic storage has its challenges, too. It requires investing in and maintaining a technology infrastructure (e.g., local area network or Web site), training people to use the technology, and dealing with administrative issues such as disaster recovery and backup.

---

1. Determine the topics requiring forms. These are topics for which he will need information throughout the project.

2. Design the forms. As with procedures and flowcharts, Perry will obtain input from the major participants. This action increases people's buy-in and their willingness to use the forms. When designing the forms, he also chooses an open layout that is easy to use.

3. Distribute a first draft of the forms. Perry gives everyone involved a chance to revise the forms and sharpen their design.

4. Perry prepares the forms in their final form, for either electronic use or as printed hard copies. Each form includes instructions on submitting the completed form and also handling changes to the form at a later date.

REPORTS

The right amount of feedback can make the difference between the success and failure of a project. Reports are vehicles for giving reliable feedback.

Reports communicate information. They help project managers monitor and track individual and overall performance, indicating when to take

Exhibit 13-7. Overall performance evaluation.

Monthly Status Report Form

Instructions: Complete each field according to the procedure "Completing the Monthly Status Report Form." Make one copy for your records and forward the original to the Program Office, Mailstop 3X-41.
Project Name: Date:

Schedule:
    Start date (baseline):
    Finish date (baseline):
    Management Estimate at Completion Date:
    Variance:

Budget:
    Original Total Cost Estimate:
    Estimated Cost to Date:
    Actual Cost to Date:
    Management Estimate at Completion Cost:
    Variance:

Overall Performance Evaluation:

corrective action. And they give feedback to everyone involved about their contributions to the project.

For reports to offer these advantages, however, they must have certain characteristics. They must:

- Be easily understood
- Be produced and available in a timely manner
- Have timely, meaningful information
- Not be too numerous

To use reports on his project, Perry performs the following seven steps:

1. He identifies the topics. Will he need reports on the schedule? Costs? Quality? Typical reports are activity relationship reports, bar charts, cost reports, histograms, network diagrams, problem reports, project status reports, and resource usage reports.

2. For each report, Perry determines information requirements and the means to collect it. He reviews the statement of work for reporting requirements, determines the readership for each report, and interviews recipients to determine their informational needs.

3. He lays out the report, keeping in mind clarity, logic, and relevancy. He remembers to keep the report simple and focuses on obtaining the information that's needed.

4. He determines the frequency of generation. Weekly? Biweekly? Monthly? Ad hoc?

5. He distributes the reports. Often, he will generate these reports via a software package on a personal computer to give him the ability to experiment with communications modes.

6. He obtains feedback. Sometimes the reports will not contain enough information; other times, they might have too much and be distracting. Because generating reports takes time and effort, he wants to minimize frustration by keeping the reports helpful and concise.

7. He stores a copy of each report, in case he needs an audit trail or to develop lessons learned in the project.

MEMOS

Many people hate to write memos. That's unfortunate, because a well-written memo can have tremendous impact on coworkers.

A memo provides a record of results. It encourages commitment to an idea or cause. It offers traceability. It raises issues and helps resolve them. Above all, memos are excellent tools for communicating with other people.

To fulfill these purposes, however, memos must be clear, concise, direct, legible, and organized. Exhibit 13-8 is an example of a well-written memo.

Perry will always prepare a memo to clarify a policy or subject, document the results of a meeting, raise an issue and get it resolved, record an accident, or schedule events. Thus, a memo should contain a date, addressee, subject, message statement, giving the who, what, when, where, and why of a subject, information on a response if desired, and signature. Memos can be prepared and sent electronically or via hard copy.

NEWSLETTERS

Not every project is big enough to warrant its own newsletter. For large projects, however, a newsletter can be invaluable.

A newsletter can enhance communications, informing everyone of important happenings and giving new information. It provides the project manager with the opportunity to "get the word out," especially about matters that directly affect project performance. It also serves as a record of

Exhibit 13-8. Example of a well-written memo.

Date: February 28, 19XX

To: Gina Davies   713-1
      Cynthia Fralusinski   714-2
      Raymond Leazowitz   713-2
      David Rockford   713-3
      Vy Toon   714-3
      Hank Wilson   715-1
      Henry Winkless   716-8

cc: Eva Brewster   716-7
      Larry Eisenberg   715-4

Subject: Planning Meeting for Bridal Shower

On March 10, we will hold a planning session for the Smythe bridal shower in the Rainbow Conference Room on the second floor of the Corporate Headquarters Building.

Prior to the meeting, prepare and bring a list of action items to share with the group.

If you have any questions or comments, please feel free to contact me at extension 4127.

Perry

Project Manager, Smythe Wedding
Mailstop 713-4

---

significant activities and accomplishments. Finally, it answers questions and dispels rumors before they arise.

There are, however, several issues related to publishing a newsletter. For example, the newsletter can become a political rather than a communications tool, serving merely to pacify political sensitivities. It is time-consuming and labor intensive to develop. Writing, proofreading, printing, and distributing a newsletter, whether in hard copy or electronic form, is no easy task. It requires, too, people who can write and edit, talents that are not too common apparently.

A newsletter can cover many topics, including team successes, challenges, biographies of participants, and new techniques developed. The key to keeping a newsletter active is to encourage team members, and the internal customer, to submit articles for the publication. That encourages people to read it and feel it is not a propaganda rag.

HISTORY FILES

During the fog of managing a project, important documentation can be lost or misplaced. To ensure that does not happen, Perry sets up project history files.

These files can be a drawer in a filing cabinet or a directory on a personal computer or file server. In any form, they provide the ability to reconstruct situations for an audit trail, review problems, and satisfy audit requirements. They help reduce the learning curve of new team members, as they review titles to become familiar with critical issues and they provide background information for further work.

Project history files frequently contain: bar charts of schedules, drafts of documents, work estimates, completed forms, memorandums, minutes of meetings, network diagrams, procedures, reports, responsibility matrices, statements of work, and work breakdown structures.

Perry must keep the files up to date, from the start to the end of the project. That's why he establishes them as early as posible. He also establishes a procedure for removing and tracking files to avoid losing or misplacing documentation. For example, he might provide a check-in/check-out sheet that people sign when removing and returning a file. He designates an area where everyone can access the files. (Often, by accident, project managers lock the files in their drawers or do not store them on the file server, thereby making accessibility difficult.) Finally, he assigns someone to maintain the files.

Perry performs four basic steps to set up project history files:

1. He identifies their contents, e.g., as being only recent sets of schedules, or all previous versions.
2. He determines their organization, e.g., by topic or date.
3. He controls their removal, e.g., by means of a check-in/check-out sheet.
4. He makes their location obvious and provides the information needed to access them, e.g., by writing an announcement and distributing it via newsletter or e-mail.

PROJECT MANUAL

It is often handy to have certain information readily available, such as phone numbers and task listings. Perry knows that a project manual can be that reference. It is an essential reference book for project management. The project manual, however, does more than provide its readers with useful information. It is also a communication tool, enabling people to interact efficiently and effectively.

Exhibit 13-9 is the table of contents for the Smythe Project manual. Of course, there is no restriction on content other than being useful, relevant, and readable.

Ideally, the manual should be prepared early on and be maintained throughout the project cycle. Everyone should have ready access to it, either in hard copy or electronic form.

To compile the project manual, Perry performs these six steps.

1. He determines the contents, e.g., by interviewing team members or reviewing the statement of work.
2. He organizes the contents, e.g., arranging them by topic or phase.
3. He determines the number of copies, e.g., by using the size of the team as the basis.
4. He assigns responsibility for maintaining the manual, e.g., to someone working on a noncritical task.
5. He publishes and distributes the manuals, e.g., electronically or as hard copy.
6. He seeks feedback from the users of the manual, e.g., by providing tear sheets on which they can submit suggestions.

THE PROJECT LIBRARY

The project library, like the history files, stores information. The major difference is that the library contains more than project management information. The project library also stores company and project-specific policies and procedures, history files, newsletters, journal publications, and related books, and technical documentation.

As he did to set up the history files, Perry follows these steps to set up the library:

1. He identifies the contents, e.g., by interviewing team members for their suggestions.
2. He determines the organization, e.g., arranging documents by title, code, or author.
3. He controls the removal of documents, e.g., by providing a check-in/check-out sheet.
4. He determines the location of the library, e.g., providing a readily accessible site; he also determines the procedures for accessing material.

DETERMINING THE PAPER TRAIL'S LENGTH

Too much or too little documentation can negatively affect a project. Perry recognizes that the key is to have the right amount of documentation to

Exhibit 13-9. Table of contents for the Smythe Project manual.

Table of Contents

I.   INTRODUCTORY SEGMENT
    A. Purpose of the manual
    B. How to use the manual
    C. Who to contact for revisions

II. PROJECT BACKGROUND INFORMATION
    A. Statement of work
    B. Project declaration

III. RESPONSIBILITIES
    A. Organization chart
    B. Job descriptions and responsibilities

IV. POLICIES, PROCEDURES, AND WORKFLOWS
    Copies relating to these topics:
        1. People
        2. Scheduling
        3. Qualities
        4. Costs
        5. Other

V.   FORMS
    Copies relating to these topics:
        1. People
        2. Scheduling
        3. Qualities
        4. Costs
        5. Other

VI. REPORTS
    Samples relating to these topics:
        1. People
        2. Scheduling
        3. Qualities
        4. Costs
        5. Other

VII. REFERENCE LISTINGS
    A. Phone listings
    B. Functional priorities
    C. Documentation matrix
    D. Other

VIII. OTHER ADMINISTRATIVE TOPICS

IX. APPENDICES

satisfy the right needs. He knows that the content of documents should be current, clear, concise, and organized to be useful to team members. He ensures, too, that the documentation is accessible to everyone, such as through a project manual or library.

Questions for Getting Started

1. If developing procedures, did you:
   - Identify the topics?
   - Determine the types of procedures needed?
   - Receive reviews by all relevant people?
   - Distribute the procedures?
   - Document the procedures?
   - Place the procedures under configuration control?
   - Seek feedback?
2. If developing flowcharts, did you:
   - Identify the topics?
   - Determine the types of diagrams to use?
   - Issue standard templates?
   - Determine whether the flowchart will supplement or replace a procedure?
   - Distribute the flowchart?
   - Seek feedback?
3. If developing forms, did you:
   - Determine what forms you need?
   - Design each form according to the characteristics described in this chapter?
   - Determine how people can obtain a copy of the form?
   - Determine how and where people can submit a completed form?
   - Institute a way for people to provide feedback on the forms?
4. If developing reports, did you:
   - Determine the necessary types of reports to use?
   - Design each report according to the characteristics described in this chapter?
   - Inform everyone who need to receive the reports?
   - Develop a distribution list?
   - Determine the frequency of generation for each report?
   - Determine where to store the reports?
   - Seek feedback from users?
5. If you need to prepare a memo, did you:
   - Include a date, subject title, address, signature block, and purpose statement?
   - Answer the who, what, when, where, and why questions?

- Check for clarity, conciseness, directives, legibility, and structure?
6. If you decide to publish a newsletter, did you determine:
   - Who will prepare the newsletter?
   - The frequency of the publication?
   - Who must review it prior to each publication?
   - The topics?
   - The layout?
   - The method of distribution?
7. If you decide to have a project manual, did you:
   - Determine the method for keeping the manual—that is, hard copy, electronic copy, Web site?
   - Determine the contents?
   - Develop a structure, reflected in the form of a table of contents?
   - Determine the number of copies?
   - Select the mode of binding?
   - Assign responsibilities for keeping the manual current?
   - Set up a format for reviewing the contents?
   - Seek feedback?
8. If you elected to set up project history files, did you:
   - Determine the contents?
   - Determine the organizational structure?
   - Assign responsibility for maintaining them?
   - Establish a procedure for accessing, removing and replacing them?
   - Communicate their location and procedure for accessing, removing, and returning them?
9. If you decide to set up a project library, did you:
   - Determine the contents?
   - Determine the filing system?
   - Assign responsibility for maintaining it?
   - Establish a procedure for accessing, removing, and replacing material?
   - Communicate the location and procedure for accessing, removing, and returning material?

Chapter 14

Team Dynamics and Successful Interactions

The organization functions of the project manager's job extend well beyond developing the team, allocating resources, estimating costs, and providing documentation. The project manager also needs to set up the elements for facilitating team dynamics—in other words, making it all work. This includes setting up a project office, holding regular meetings, making presentations, and using people skills to encourage team members to reach the project goal.

SET UP THE PROJECT OFFICE

Since his project is comparatively large and has high visibility, Perry sets up a project office. Despite employing a Web site and other computer technologies for communications, he'll need a central location to manage the efforts.

Perry's ideal office has telephones, fax, and other communications equipment, as well as storage space for hard-copy forms, the history files, and the project library. Since the project office will also be a meeting place for team members, it has cubicles for working and conference rooms to hold meetings, training sessions, and other project-related activities. There is equipment such as easel stands, overhead projector with extra bulbs, screen, whiteboards, and tables with a sufficient number of chairs. In addition, the project office has tape, writing instruments, paper, viewfoils, sticky notes, paper clips, easel pads, and the like.

While this all sounds like common sense, the reality is that many projects, even those with a project office, lack such simple resources. Some advance planning in this regard can make managing the project much smoother.

Often overlooked, too, is the realization that the project office is a communications center. It is like a computer network control center where all information flows in and out. In this communications center is a very important tool, called a *visibility wall* or *visibility room*. This wall or room is where all project documentation is showcased. Perry puts on the walls of his visibility room his bar charts, maps, minutes of key meetings, network diagrams, organization charts, photographs (e.g., recognition awards), process flows, responsibility matrices, statements of work, technical drawings, and work breakdown structures. Essentially, what goes on the walls depends on what Perry deems important for everyone to see.

When setting up a visibility room, Perry remembers the following points.

1. Plan in advance. On a sheet of paper, Perry draws a picture of what goes on which wall. This prevents rework and reduces costs, especially if he is using high-quality graphics.
2. Keep the walls current. This way people have a reason to review the walls. The walls serve no purpose if no one looks at them.
3. Use the walls. Perry will hold meetings in the room and refer to the items posted; his actions enforce the importance of the information on the walls.

CONDUCT MEETINGS

There will be meetings frequently, and they will consume a large percentage of everyone's time. These meetings are usually one of three basic types: checkpoint reviews, status reviews, and staff meetings. In addition, there are occasional ad hoc meetings.

The *checkpoint review* is held at specific points in time, usually after a red-letter day or significant event (e.g., completion of a major milestone). Its purpose is to determine what has been done and decide whether to proceed or cancel the project. Exhibit 14-1 is an agenda from one of Perry's checkpoint reviews.

The purpose of the *status review* is to collect information to determine progress in satisfying cost, schedule, and quality criteria. The status review is held regularly (e.g., weekly or biweekly). Exhibit 14-2 is an agenda from one of Perry's status reviews.

Like the status review, the *staff meeting* is held regularly. All team members receive information from the project manager and share additional data and insights. Exhibit 14-3 is an agenda from one of Perry's staff meetings.

The *ad hoc meeting* is held irregularly, often spontaneously by team members. The idea is to resolve an issue or communicate information. Exhibit 14-4 is an agenda from one of the Smythe Project's many ad hoc meetings.

Whether conducting a staff meeting, status review, checkpoint review,

Exhibit 14-1. Checkpoint review agenda.

Agenda

April 7, 19XX

I.   Background
    A. Previous red-letter events/milestones
    B. Challenge in the past

II. Lessons regarding this event
    A. Achievements/successes
    B. Problems and challenges
    C. Remaining issues

III. Decision whether to proceed as is, differently, or halt

IV. Remaining issues

V.   Open forum

Exhibit 14-2. Status review agenda.

Agenda

February 28, 19XX

I.   Input to status regarding:
    A. Schedule
    B. Budget
    C. Quality

II. Issues and concerns regarding:
    A. Schedule
    B. Budget
    C. Quality
    D. Other

III. Open forum

IV. Next meeting

Exhibit 14-3. Staff meeting agenda.

Agenda

March 3, 19XX

I. Information
    A. Announcements
    B. Issues of concern
        ▪ Schedule
        ▪ Quality
        ▪ Budget
        ▪ Other
    C. Recognition
    D. Upcoming issues and events
    E. Open Forum
    F. Next Meeting

---

or ad hoc meeting, Perry applies five rules to ensure efficient and effective meetings.

1. Prepare an agenda. He will follow an agenda like the ones in Exhibits 14-1 through 14-4. An agenda is a logical listing of topics to cover. It keeps the meeting focused and ensures that it is productive.

2. Announce the meeting. He notifies attendees about the meeting in advance. Even if it is an ad hoc meeting, he informs people about the purpose of the meeting.

3. Be prepared. He comes with the right supplies, equipment, and copies of documents to distribute. This way there's no last-minute searches for equipment or extra copies.

4. Encourage participation. He gives everyone the opportunity to contribute, but avoids letting anyone dominate the meeting. He makes sure the meeting doesn't become a platform for someone's pontification, including himself.

5. Take notes and distribute the minutes afterwards. By taking notes and converting them into minutes, he communicates the importance of the meeting and increases the likelihood of people honoring their commitments.

GIVE EFFECTIVE PRESENTATIONS

Perry and his team will be giving presentations, either among themselves, to senior management, or to the customer. These presentations require

Exhibit 14-4. Ad hoc meeting agenda.

Agenda

June 11, 19XX

I. Description of situation or problem
    A. Previous red-letter events/milestones

II. Background details
    A. Who
    B. What
    C. When
    D. Where
    E. Why
    F. How

III. Alternative courses of action

IV. Select appropriate course of action

V. Plan to implement course of action
    A. Who
    B. What
    C. When
    D. Where
    E. Why
    F. How

VI. Follow-up meeting

more than standing in front of people and talking. They involve communicating.

Perry will likely have to give three fundamental types of presentations. The first is a presentation to *persuade.* He will, for example, probably have to convince senior management to provide more resources. The second type of presentation is to *inform.* He will probably have to communicate information, for example, to senior managers about cost and schedule performance. And the third type is to *explain.* For example, he might have to instruct people on project management tools and techniques.

Of course, team members will likely have to give the same types of presentations. Whether you are a project manager or team member, as a presenter you must follow six fundamental steps:

1. *Know yourself and the audience.* Find out about the audience to ascertain your commonalities and differences. You can get useful informa-

tion, for example, by interviewing people who know audience members. Follow up by making a list of what you share and don't share with the audience. This knowledge will prove useful in preparing the presentation.

2. *Perceive your audience and how it perceives you.* Look at ways to influence the audience to see you in a favorable light. This will make it easier to communicate your message. You can win the audience over, for example, by expressing values or experiences you share with its members.

3. *Determine the type and structure of the presentation.* Answer all the who, what, when, where, and why questions pertaining to your topic. Determine if your presentation is meant to inform, persuade, or explain. Then formulate your overall strategy to achieve the goal of your presentation, and your tactics for executing that strategy.

4. *Develop the material.* Build your presentation. Determine the content and logically arrange it. For example, you can arrange topics chronologically or by level of importance. Also incorporate visual aids, statistics, and other materials.

5. *Rehearse.* Practice as if you were actually giving the presentation—do a dry run. Try to improve your delivery. This is also the time to become familiar with the location for the presentation—room size, lighting, sound equipment, and so on. Rehearse there, if you can.

6. *Deliver the presentation.* You have polished your delivery, eliminated any poorly designed visual aids and distracting mannerisms (e.g., pacing about with your hands in your pockets or playing with pocket change). You should encourage and be prepared to answer questions. You might elicit questions from a reluctant audience by asking a question yourself.

APPLY INTERPERSONAL SKILLS

Interpersonal skills, also called people skills, play an integral part in the success of every project. Whatever gets accomplished is done by people and their interactions, so interpersonal skills can seriously impact results.

Interpersonal relations embrace three primary skills: being an active listener, reading people, and dealing with conflicts effectively.

Being an Active Listener

One of the best communication tools a project manager can have is *active* listening. It means listening genuinely to what the speaker is saying—in short, focusing on what is said and how it is said.

Active listeners:

- Avoid interrupting the person except to clarify a point.
- Give listening cues (e.g., nod the head or use an expression) to indicate involvement in the conversation.
- Are not preoccupied with something else during the conversation (e.g., working on documentation while the other person talks).
- Do not change the topic abruptly during the conversation.
- Do not daydream while the other person talks.
- Pay as much attention to body language as to the oral message.
- Remove all distractions (e.g., radio playing in the background).

The key is to be active, not passive, by becoming fully engaged in what is being said.

Reading People

It would be nice to know the true motives of people; however, that is impossible, since many people are not open and honest. Project managers, therefore, must identify the real issues and motivations of people.

Fortunately, there are tools to help project managers understand the motivations of people. Unfortunately, these tools do not always work, owing to the vagaries of human nature. Still, many project managers find them useful.

One tool is the *Myers-Briggs Type Indicator* for personality preferences. This identifies personality types based on a combination of four preferences: extrovert (outward) versus introvert (inward), sensing (actual) versus intuitive (sixth sense), thinking (structuring information) versus feeling (personal), and judging (organized) versus perceiving (spontaneous). These categories are useful, but require a good understanding of the preferences.

This approach does not specify which personality is better or worse or which one is good or bad. It states only that people have a preference that is reflected in the way they deal with reality, their environment, and their relationships. An excellent resource for using this indicator is *Please Understand Me: Character and Temperament Types,* by David Keirsey and Marilyn Bates.

Another popular tool is Abraham Maslow's *hierarchy of needs,* described in Chapter 4. This model is easier to use, since it identifies people's needs according to hierarchical order: physiological (food), safety (shelter), social (acceptance), esteem (sense of importance), and self-actualization (becoming). The satisfaction, or lack of earlier needs, dictates the motivations of people.

Another popular, though less widespread, personality tool is Robert

---

Transactional Analysis

Transactional analysis, or TA, describes how people interact with each other via ego states. An ego state is a combination of feelings and experiences that manifest themselves in the way people consistently behave. Essentially, behavior reflects one's feelings and experiences.

TA posits three ego states: parent, child, and adult.

- The parent ego state reflects parental feelings and experiences, like being critical and directive.
- The adult ego state reflects being realistic and objective when dealing with people.
- The child ego state reflects childlike behavior, like trying to please, uncontrollable laughter, or rebelliousness.

The interaction between two people reflects a transaction. There are several types of transactions between people, with some being parent-to-parent, parent-to-child, and parent-to-adult. Such transactions can be detected through body language and verbally.

An excellent book on TA is *Born to Win: Transactional Analysis with Gestalt Experiments,* by Muriel James and Dorothy Jongeward (Reading, Mass.: Addison Wesley, 1987).

Bolton's *social style matrix.* Bolton divides social styles and personal expectations into two dimensions: assertiveness and responsiveness. Assertiveness is the energy or effort individuals invest in influencing others. Responsiveness is the energy or effort individuals invest in controlling their emotions when dealing with other people. The combination of assertiveness and responsiveness creates social stereotypes: analytical (logical), driver (determined), amiable (diplomatic), and expressive (spontaneous). Bolton's topology does not say which social style is better or worse, or which one is good or bad. It simply states that people have to deal with life in general and social environments in particular. For more information, see *Social Style/Management Style* by Robert and Dorothy Bolton.

There are, of course, a plethora of theories about people and how to understand them, from Sigmund Freud and Carl Jung to B. F. Skinner and Frederick Herzberg. The key is to find a model or tool that works best for you, then apply it in your own circumstances.

An interesting and often reliable side concept about people is their body language. According to motivational experts, our body language reveals more about us than what we say. Some experts estimate that body language makes up 70 to 90 percent of a conversation. This means you need to pay attention to facial expressions, body movements, posture, and eye movements. A mastery of the art of reading body language can help the project manager discern whether people are truly committed to the project or providing honest status information.

There are two caveats about relying on body language. The first is to look at body language in totality—that is, avoid relying on one body movement alone. The other is that cultural differences can mislead in the interpretation of true motivations. In some cultures, for instance, it is acceptable behavior to stand closer together or to maintain eye contact while in others it is not. A misinterpretation can result in real problems. Perry keeps this thought in mind, since the Smythe wedding will occur in Italy; body language in Italy can have entirely different meanings from that in the United States.

Deal With Conflict Effectively

Conflict is a way of life and it can surface anytime during the project cycle. Conflict can arise over sharing people, equipment, supplies, or money; over goals and specifications; between personalities; over differences of opinion; and even over power.

The potential for conflict is highest, however, at the beginning, when a project manager competes for resources or when difficulties arise over contractual requirements. And conflict at the beginning can lead to even more difficulties later if it is not addressed properly. The potential for conflict is high, too, at the end of the cycle, when participants face schedule pressures. Conflict in and of itself is not bad. It can alert project managers to problems that must be addressed. The challenge is to manage the conflict in a manner that leads to project success rather than failure.

Project managers, like all people, deal with conflict differently. Some project managers avoid it, letting it smolder. Some project managers give up every time a conflict surfaces. Other project managers deny that conflict exists at all. And some masterfully blame others. These are all defense mechanisms. Nevertheless, they do not deal with the conflict. All these mechanisms manage to do is avoid conflict or push it into the background.

The question, then, is how to deal with conflict constructively. Since it really centers on people, it makes sense to view conflict as primarily a people issue. Perry takes several actions to respond to conflict.

1. He diffuses the charged emotion within himself. If he has to, he will do something as simple as count to ten before doing anything.

2. He diffuses the charged emotions in other people. He will calm down people by calling for a cooling-off period, especially when emotions run high.

3. He identifies the facts of the situation to determine the cause of the conflict. He avoids comments that can be viewed as taking sides or being accusational.

4. He applies active listening. He listens for the facts to acquire an objective assessment of the situation. Active listening helps to avoid being "pulled into" the conflict.

5. He acknowledges any anger that may be present, while focusing on the merits of the conflict. If anger is justified, he acknowledges it.

6. He keeps everyone focused on the cause of the conflict. He avoids the tendency to blame someone or to rationalize it away.

7. He keeps the big picture in focus. He asks himself what the best way is to resolve the conflict so as to achieve the project goal.

8. He sets a plan for resolving the conflict. He also remains objective.

9. He seeks participation in the resolution. Unless an impasse occurs, he lets the people decide on a mutually agreeable solution. That builds bridges and commitment to the solution.

10. He encourages a win-win solution, not a win-lose or lose-lose. With a win-win solution, emotions will subside and there will be little or no room for bitterness.

Handling Difficult People

Project managers work under pressure, with little formal authority over people. Dealing with difficult people under such circumstances just adds stress as they try to bring their projects in on time and within budget.

If that were not enough, project managers must deal with different types of difficult people. In his superb book *Coping with Difficult People* (New York: Dell Publishing, 1981), Dr. Robert Bramson identifies what he calls the hostile aggressive, compleat complainer, clam, super-agreeable, negativist, bulldozer, balloon, and staller.

In the project environment, all these categories of difficult people are present.

The hostile aggressive, for example, likes to "shoot holes" in any schedule proposal. The super-agreeable agrees to perform a task by a certain date but changes his mind based on who he talked with last. The staller is the customer who is required to make a decision and takes forever, causing the project to be delayed.

GETTING TEAMWORK TO WORK

How people on a team interact can influence the results of a project. Setting up an adequate project office contributes to effective teamwork in any project-oriented team. In addition, good communication and interpersonal skills, and effective use of conflict management techniques can go a long way toward producing positive results for a project. Perry realizes, however, that the responsibility lies with everyone to exercise positive team dynamics throughout the life of the project.

Questions for Getting Started

1. If setting up a project office, did you:
    - Develop a layout?
    - Determine the contents?
    - Determine the location?
    - Determine who will work there?
    - Determine the necessary equipment and supplies?
2. If setting up a visibility wall or room, did you:
    - Develop a layout?
    - Determine the contents?
    - Determine its purpose?
3. If holding checkpoint review meetings, did you:
    - Decide to have agendas?
    - Determine the locations?
    - Determine how to notify attendees?
    - Decide to have minutes taken?
    - Determine the necessary equipment and supplies?
    - Make an effort to get everyone's participation?
    - Determine length of the meetings?
4. If holding status review meetings, did you:
    - Decide to have agendas?
    - Determine the locations?
    - Determine how to notify attendees?
    - Decide to have minutes taken?
    - Determine the necessary equipment and supplies?
    - Make an effort to get everyone's participation?
    - Determine length of the meetings?
5. If holding staff meetings, did you:
    - Decide to have agendas?
    - Determine the locations?
    - Determine how to notify attendees?
    - Decide to have minutes taken?
    - Determine the necessary equipment and supplies?

- Make an effort to get everyone's participation?
- Determine length of the meetings?

6. If holding ad hoc meetings, did you:
   - Decide to have agendas?
   - Determine the locations?
   - Determine how to notify attendees?
   - Decide to have minutes taken?
   - Determine the necessary equipment and supplies?
   - Make an effort to get everyone's participation?
   - Determine length of the meetings?

7. If giving presentations, did you:
   - Determine the types to give?
   - Determine your audience?
   - Recognize the key perceptions?
   - Prepare the logical structure?
   - Develop clean, meaningful material?
   - Rehearse?
   - Give a successful delivery?

8. Are you an active listener?

9. Can you "read people"? Do you need a way to do that? What is that way?

10. How well do you deal with conflict? What approach do you take to deal with it? On an individual basis? On a team basis?

Chapter 15

Performance Assessment: Tracking and Monitoring

With a solid project definition, plan, and organizational infrastructure, Perry is confident that he can control his project. He is not naïve enough, however, to think that he can sit back and remain idle. Quite the contrary, he knows all about Murphy's law. He knows from the physicist's view of the universe that entropy can occur.

So he responds—not reacts—to changing circumstances. He does that best by tracking and monitoring performance. And the keys to tracking and monitoring performance are status data and status assessments.

COLLECT STATUS DATA

Status data offer several advantages for Perry. From the data he can determine project performance—specifically, how well the goals of the project are being met. He can also determine how efficiently work is being done. He can reduce his and everyone else's frustration and anxiety by providing feedback. It instills confidence in everyone that the project is under control, that the project manager is monitoring its pulse. Finally, he can maintain communications and information sharing among the participants.

Unfortunately, status data are often not collected well. The task can be labor intensive and time-consuming. This is especially the case when there is no previous infrastructure in place or when the team members lack experience. If the project manager, or the team, lacks the expertise or knowledge of collection, there may be an inappropriate assessment. Also, the project team may be using incompatible computing tools and converting the data requires considerable effort and expertise. Teams using older software and hardware particularly find this situation complicates data collection.

The style of the project manager can affect data collection. If she prefers to "shoot from the hip" or rely less on administration, the project manager will likely rely more on intuition and informal methods for data collection. Though there's some merit under certain circumstances, this can result in gross misjudgments. Likewise, the project manager may not have a good grasp of the project's scope. Failure to understand the scope can result in problems determining what data are needed.

Perry, fortunately, is not one of these project managers. He understands the importance of reliable data. He must have certain prerequisites in place to do meaningful assessments.

- A solid information infrastructure. He sets up a process for identifying, collecting, and compiling data that will be reliable and valid.

- Available expertise. He assigns responsibility for collecting data to someone who has a good understanding of data collection techniques.

- A standardized set of tools to collect and compile the data. He knows that a mixture of incompatible hardware and software will cause frustration levels to rise and nobody, not even himself, will bother to collect data.

- Clear value in collecting data. If people do not see the value of data collection, they will be reluctant to expend the effort. Collecting data must be meaningful on both individual and group levels. This distinction is important, since it affects how the data will eventually be formatted and reported.

Methods of Collection

Perry uses formal and informal modes for collecting data. *Formal modes* include status reviews, one-on-one sessions, and forms.

The status review, discussed in Chapter 13, is held regularly. The meeting covers cost, schedule, and quality measures. Perry collects data prior to the status review, so that at the meeting he can discuss the current status, make an assessment, and determine corrective actions. With proper technology, he could, at the meeting, enter the data into a computer, generate the necessary reports, assess the program, and decide an appropriate action to take.

There are problems with collecting data at status review meetings. For example, sometimes the meetings can skew results. Peer pressure can directly or indirectly force people to fudge the data in order to paint an optimistic or pessimistic picture. It is also important to remember that while collecting status data, the project manager remain objective and not influence the reports. The project manager must hear what he needs to hear and not what he wants to hear. Biased data lead to biased assessments.

One-on-one sessions work best for collecting data just prior to a status review. The project manager or her representatives meet with each person individually to collect status data.

But as the number of team members increases, so does the time needed to collect data and, as time passes by, the data age. Also, the data collected in one-on-one sessions could be more subjective than if gathered in a group setting. If peer pressure does not overtake a status meeting, more objective data will likely be available as people question the reports.

Forms are another way to collect data. Team members complete the forms with status data and submit them to the project office for processing. The data are then compiled. Ideally, the forms are computer-based and team members can forward them electronically for quick, easy compilation.

Collecting data on forms presents a challenge, however. Getting the forms submitted on time is one problem, since some people often procrastinate. The other is that forms may get lost. Both problems grow in magnitude as the number of team members gets larger.

Informal modes of data collection include holding ad hoc sessions, using word of mouth, and relying on your own judgment regarding status. Informal modes are quicker and involve less administrative hassles; they are the path of least resistance. But the data collected may not be objective, resulting in a greater chance of error. Still, many project managers rely on informal methods.

Perry decides to use both formal and informal modes of data collection. He uses status reviews to verify the accuracy of the data collected in one-on-one sessions and via forms. But he also keeps his ears open for additional information.

Data Validity and Reliability

When collecting data, Perry keeps two main concepts in mind: reliability and validity. *Reliability* implies consistent results—in other words, does the data yield reliable results? *Validity* involves the approach or tool used to collect data. Does it influence the results, thereby introducing bias, which in turn slants the results?

Some validity errors include inconsistent application of measurement tools, failing to account for changing circumstances, using a collection tool that guarantees a particular result, and undue influence by the personality of the data collector. These are threats to data validity because they influence the data being inputted and the information being derived.

There are other examples of how collection efforts can negatively influence data reliability and validity.

- The "90 percent syndrome." Team members say they have 90 percent completed a task; for its remainder, it stays 90 percent complete. Then the task slides past its completion date. Of course, the problem is that the last 10 percent proves the most difficult.

- The Hawthorne effect. What was accomplished just prior to collection influences a person's estimate of the amount of work done. The problem is that what was done last may not be significant, giving a misleading impression.

- Overly negative or positive data. Some team members always exaggerate, saying too much or too little has been done.

- The "good news" effect. Some team members tell the project manager what she wants to hear, usually good news. Hence, the project manager does not get a balanced view.

- Lies. Rather than give honest data, some people lie, figuring perhaps no one will know or the project manager will eventually leave before anyone finds out.

Faulty data collection can have a big impact on project performance. Garbage in, garbage out: the quality of output is only as good as the quality of input. Good data lead to good decision making; bad data lead to poor decision making.

ASSESS STATUS

With reliable and valid data, Perry can assess overall project performance. Assessment involves determining how well the project has and will achieve its goals. Perry focuses on three areas: schedule, cost, and quality.

Perry assesses status via two principal reviews, looking back (history) and looking forward (the future). Looking at past performance is called *tracking*; projecting into the future using past performance is called *monitoring*. Both are important for determining where the project has been and where it will be if the current level of performance continues.

A key concept behind assessing status is *variance,* the difference between what is planned and what has actually occurred up to a specific point. The formula is quite simple:

$$\text{Variance} = \text{planned} - \text{actual}$$

If the difference between the two is zero or a positive number, then the project is proceeding as expected, whether from a cost, schedule, or quality perspective. If the difference between the planned and the actual is a negative number, then the project is not progressing as anticipated. Quality variance is discussed in Chapter 16; the remainder of this chapter deals with cost and schedule variances.

It is important to note, however, that variance is a deviation from what is expected. The deviation in itself may not necessarily mean something is wrong—it can indicate something good, too. A variance is a signal to investigate the situation and determine whether to take action.

Determining Variance

The tracking portion of the variance calculation is the *actual to date*. The monitoring portion is the *estimate at completion*; it is based on actual progress to date plus the remainder of work to do, assuming the current rate of progress is maintained.

Cost variance is calculated by using this equation:

$$\text{Cost variance} = \text{budgeted cost} - \text{actual cost}$$

The equation result tells Perry whether he has spent more money than planned up to a specific point in time. He calculates it for each task, which in turn is accumulated to give the total estimate at completion for the entire project. A positive value is called an *underrun* and a negative one is called an *overrun*. Exhibit 15-1 shows examples of cost variances on the Smythe Project.

Exhibit 15-1. Cost variances.

Smythe Project Budget Sheet $ in Thousands April 16, _____						
Task	Budget to Date	Actual to Date	Under-run	Over-run	Total Budget	Estimate at Completion
6.1.1.1 Identify limousine service to church	168	360		192	840	1,032
6.1.1.2 Coordinate limousine service to church	56	104		48	280	328
6.1.1.3 Identify limousine service to reception	168	110	58		840	782
6.1.1.4 Coordinate limousine service to reception	56	124		68	280	348

Schedule variance follows the same pattern. It is the difference between planned and actual start and end dates, respectively. This variance
tells Perry whether he has spent more time than planned on a task up to a
specific point in time. He calculates it for each task, which in turn is accumulated to give the total estimate at completion for the entire project. A
positive value represents an ahead-of-schedule condition while a negative
one represents a behind-schedule situation. Exhibit 15-2 has some examples from the Smythe Project.

Earned Value

In the previous section, cost and schedule variances were treated indepen-
dently. There is, however, a way to treat them as an integrated entity, called
earned value. It is the preferred way to measure project performance.

Earned value consists of three basic variables:

Exhibit 15-2. Project schedule sheet.

Smythe Project Schedule Sheet April 16, ____						
Task	Early Start	Early Finish	Dur-ation (days)	Actual Start	Actual Finish	Estimate at Completion
6.1.1.1 Identify limousine service to church	April 1	April 3	3	April 2	April 5	April 5
6.1.1.2 Coordinate limousine service to church	April 7	April 7	1	April 9		April 11
6.1.2.1 Determine transportation requirements to church	April 4	April 6	3	April 6	April 7	April 7
6.1.2.2 Coordinate transportation to church	April 7	April 8	2	April 7		
6.1.2.5 Arrange for valet service for church	April 9	April 9	1			

- *Budgeted cost for work scheduled*
- *Budgeted cost for work performed*
- *Actual cost of work performed*

The budgeted cost for work scheduled (BCWS) is the estimated cost for a task, or group of tasks, that are scheduled to be performed for a specific time period. In other words, it is the estimated value of the work scheduled. The budgeted cost for work performed (BCWP) is the estimated cost that is approved for a task or group of tasks, to be completed up to a specific period of time. In other words, it is the estimated value of the work completed up to a specific point in time. The actual cost of work performed (ACWP) is the actual costs accrued for a task, or group of tasks, up to a specific point in time.

The BCWS, BCWP, and ACWP are all instrumental in calculating the cost variance (CV) and the schedule variance (SV), which in turn are used to assess individual and project performance. Here are the calculations for both:

$$CV = BCWP - ACWP$$
$$SV = BCWP - BCWS$$

For the Smythe Project example (using $ in thousands):

CV = 200 (or BCWP) − 300 (or ACWP) = − 100, indicating a cost overrun
SV = 200 (or BCWP) − 220 (or BCWS) = − 20, indicating behind schedule

For ease of calculation, the best approach is to convert the cost variance and schedule variance to percentages:

$$CV \% = (BCWP - ACWP) / BCWP$$
$$SV \% = (BCWP - BCWS) / BCWS$$

For the Smythe Project example (using $ in thousands):

$$
\begin{aligned}
CV \% &= (BCWP - ACWP) / BCWP \\
&= (200 - 300) / 200 \\
&= -50\%, \text{ indicating a cost overrun} \\
SV \% &= (BCWP - BCWS) / BCWS \\
&= (200 - 220) / 220 \\
&= -9\%, \text{ indicating the task is behind schedule}
\end{aligned}
$$

The values are then plotted cumulatively over time for all three variables as shown in Exhibit 15-3. Again, this can be performed for one task or the entire project.

After calculating the BCWS, BCWP, and the ACWP, Perry can deter-

Exhibit 15-3. Earned value.

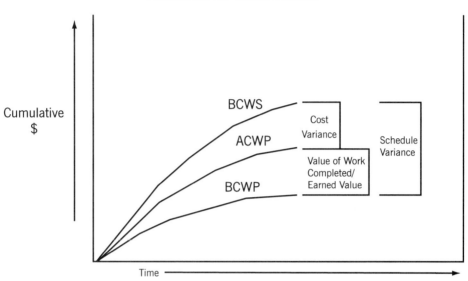

mine in what combination of the following circumstances he might find the project:

BCWP = BCWS	On Schedule
BCWP < BCWS	Behind Schedule
BCWP > BCWS	Ahead of Schedule
BCWP = ACWP	Meeting Cost Target
BCWP < ACWP	Cost Overrun
BCWP > ACWP	Cost Underrun

The BCWS, BCWP, and ACWP also are useful for determining overall project performance. The measures for doing so are the cost performance index (CPI) and the schedule performance index (SPI), which are calculated as:

CPI = BCWP / ACWP or planned costs / actual costs
SPI = BCWP / BCWS or planned costs / scheduled costs

Smythe Project example ($ in thousands):

CPI = BCWP / ACWP
   = 200 / 300 = .66, indicating cost performance is not very
      efficient since the result is less than 1.00
SPI = BCWP / BCWS
   = 200 / 220 = .91, indicating schedule performance is not
      very efficient since the result is less than 1.00

The measure of performance is determined by how close the calculated value approximates 1.00. If the CPI and SPI are less than 1.00, then performance needs improvement. If greater than 1.00, then performance exceeds expectations. This can be performed for one, a group, or all tasks on the project.

MAKING PERFORMANCE ASSESSMENT COUNT

A project plan serves no purpose if no one knows or cares if it is being followed. Perry, therefore, regularly keeps a "pulse" on the schedule and cost performance of the project. He collects and analyzes data to ensure that plan and reality match as closely as possible. If a variance exists, he determines whether to take corrective action. Of course, a variance can exist for quality as much as it does for cost and schedule. Perry knows that and ensures that metrics also exist to measure quality.

Questions for Getting Started

1. When collecting data for determining cost and schedule status, did you determine:
   - Expertise needed?
   - Mode of collection (e.g., formal versus informal)?
   - Obstacles you will face?
   - Tools to do the job?
   - Type of information infrastructure you want in place?
   - Ways to communicate the value of collecting status?
2. In regard to status reviews, did you determine whether to collect data prior to or during the meetings?
3. When collecting data, did you identify the threats to reliability? To validity? How will you deal with those threats?
4. When assessing status, what variables will you look at? Variances? Cost variance? Schedule variance? Earned value? How will you go about calculating them and how often? Will the calculations be for selected tasks or the entire project?

Chapter 16
Quality Assessment: Metrics

In Chapter 15, Perry developed ways to assess performance with regard to cost and schedule variances. Quality assessment is the other element in monitoring performance.

Establishing measurements for quality is a way to identify opportunities to reduce waste, determine how the project is achieving its goals, ascertain trends, and establish baselines for future projects.

Quality can have several meanings, so Perry defines the word in terms of his project. After consulting the customer and reviewing project documentation (the statement of work), he defines quality as service that satisfies a defined degree of excellence. In terms of the Smythe Project, quality is satisfying the requirements set by the Smythe family. Focusing on his customer's requirements, Perry can determine the measurements to use. *Metrics* are the tools and techniques he will use to track and assess quality.

INTRODUCTION TO METRICS

There are two basic categories of metrics, qualitative and quantitative. *Qualitative metrics* are intangible, noncalibrated measures. Examples include degree of customer satisfaction and degree of importance. These metrics are subjective. *Quantitative metrics* are tangible, calibrated measures. Examples include financial analysis and parametrics. These metrics are objective.

Qualitative and quantitative metrics can be used to measure the satisfaction of the customer's requirements, as well as the efficiency and effectiveness of processes for building a product or delivering a service. In their simplest form, quality metrics measure the relationship between the number of errors and a unit of measure. An error is the difference between what is expected and what has occurred—in other words, a variance.

Of course, Perry knows that metrics do not happen spontaneously. He must set up a process for collecting data, then analyzing the results. So Perry takes the following actions.

1. He determines what to measure. The statement of work provides much information; however, he also interviews the customer and examines the metrics used for earlier projects of a similar nature.

2. He seeks agreement on what metrics to use. There are quantitative and qualitative metrics, simple and complex. People must see the value of a metric; otherwise, they will not support the collection efforts or respect the results.

3. He obtains the software to perform the metrics. These include project management software, database applications, and modeling packages.

THE COLLECTION AND ANALYSIS OF DATA

Perry must build a good database. Without data he cannot do much. If the data lack reliability and validity, they produce useless results. But having good project management disciplines in place will help in collecting reliable, valid data. Perry has the expertise to collect good data, including statistical knowledge, analytical prowess, and communications skills. Without these skills, establishing the metrics would be extremely difficult. Also, Perry must exercise discipline when implementing the metrics. This means collecting data regularly and using comparable methods over time.

Perry follows five steps to measure quality: (1) identifying what needs to be measured, (2) collecting the data, (3) compiling the data, (4) analyzing the data, and (5) communicating the results.

Identify the Measures

As noted earlier, there are multiple ways to identify what needs to be measured. Perry reviews project and technical documentation. He meets with people directly as well as remotely connected to the project. He reviews the history of similar projects. He selects benchmarks, or examples from other companies against which to compare his results. In any event, he must have buy-in for whatever methods he chooses. Without buy-in, support may decline.

Of course, the audience will largely dictate what metrics to use. The project team may want to measure technical aspects. Senior management and the customer may want measurements of customer satisfaction. Perry is interested in measuring his project management. In any question of determinants, business considerations should be first. Ultimately, customer satisfaction is the quality metric.

A way to determine business metrics is to identify key project indicators, or KPI. These are elements of a project that contribute to successful completion of a project. On the Smythe Project, a KPI is the number of complaints about the bridal shower. To identify KPIs, determine all the

PDCA

A useful concept for performing metrics is the *Plan, Do, Check, Act* cycle, also known as the PDCA Wheel or the Deming Wheel.

The *Plan* is developing an approach for improving a process or implementing a metric or both. The *Do* is turning the plan into reality by executing it. The *Check* is determining if the improvement or metric is working. The *Act* is making any changes to improve the process or metric. The cycle is shown below.

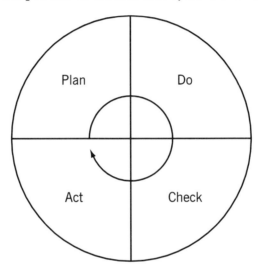

This cycle repeats throughout the process or measurement; it ensures stepwise refinement of the plan.

In reality, the PDCA cycle can be applied to any decision-making endeavor. Managing a project lends itself to application of the PDCA cycle; project plans are continually revised to reflect reality.

processes involved in project management, process management, and technical performance. Then, with selected representatives, rank those processes and select the most important top ten.

Whatever the metrics chosen, Perry answers the following questions for each measurement tool:

- Who is the metric for?
- What purpose will it serve?

- How often will the measurement be taken?
- What is the formula?
- What is the data source?

Collect the Data

Perry uses data from the project data repository created by his project management software. He ensures the data are current, thanks to input from status review.

In addition to the data repository, he searches the project history files and project library for relevant data. He can access completed forms, past reports, and memos. He also uses alternative sources like the Internet for data in the public domain and available through think tanks.

Compile the Data

Perry must put the data into a usable format. One of his first actions is to cleanse the data, identifying bad (irrelevant) data and standardizing it (putting it into the same format). Perry sorts the data, reviews it to determine any anomalies (e.g., alphabetic characters in a numeric field) and ensures that it has all the decimal points in the right place. While doing this, he avoids introducing bias, which would influence the results. For example, he removes data to which he might respond subjectively, such as data originating from a person or system that he dislikes.

Data are raw, while information is data in a meaningful form. Perry has several tools to convert data into information, including Pareto charts, checksheets, scattergrams, histograms, control charts, and trend charts.

Pareto charts display information to determine the potential causes of a problem. A bar chart (not a Gantt chart) shows the major categories or elements on the x-axis and the prioritized numbers of a result (e.g., number of complaints) on the y-axis, as shown in Exhibit 16-1. The highest bar has the greatest likelihood of being the cause of the problem.

Checksheets are documents that record the frequency of distribution of incidents. Each occurrence is recorded in an interval identified, as shown in Exhibit 16-2. The information identifies what intervals have the greatest and least number of occurrences. The checksheet also graphically displays information in the form of a histogram, as shown in Exhibit 16-3.

Scattergrams, sometimes called scatter or correlation charts, show the relationship between two variables, as shown in Exhibit 16-4. Normal relationships are "bunched together"; the abnormal relationships are "outside the bunch," thereby indicating an anomalous situation.

Control charts, like the scattergrams, identify normal and anomalous

Exhibit 16-1. Pareto chart example.

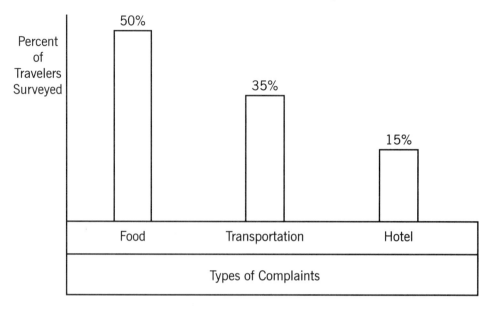

Exhibit 16-2. Checksheet example.

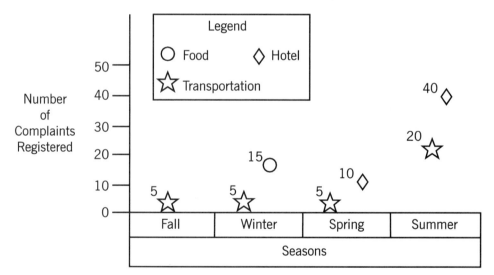

situations, specifically variance from the average. Upper permissible and lower levels of variation are identified. As with the scattergram, the focus in on variation, with emphasis on reducing erratic behavior. To better understand control charts, here's an example for building one.

Six hotels are interested in knowing the average number of complaints during the summer season. The analyst collects data from these six hotels and compiles them in the table on pages 157 and 158.

Exhibit 16-3. Histogram example.

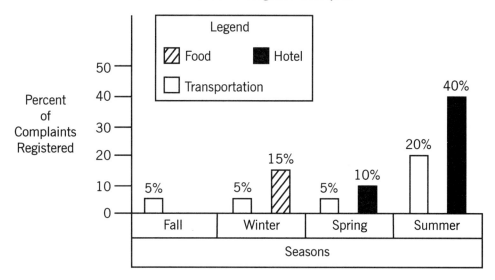

Exhibit 16-4. Scattergram example.

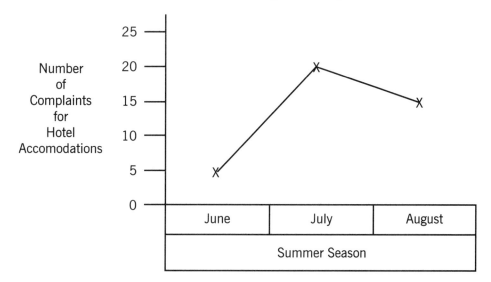

Hotel	Average Number of Complaints
A	30
B	40
C	60
D	80

Hotel	Average Number of Complaints
E	35
F	25
	270

Before drawing the control chart, the analyst determines the "average average," and the upper and lower limits of the control chart. The "average average" is the sum of the averages divided by the sample size, or N (the number of hotels participating); thus, 270 divided by 6 equals 45. See the control chart in Exhibit 16-5 for a plotted graph.

The equation for the upper control limit is

$$\overline{\overline{X}} + \frac{3 * \text{standard deviation}}{\sqrt{N}} \quad \text{where } \overline{\overline{X}} \text{ is the "average average"}$$
$$= 45 + (3*19.1)/2.5$$
$$= 67.9 \text{ for the upper control limit.}$$

For the lower control limit, the equation is:

$$\overline{\overline{X}} + \frac{3 * \text{standard deviation}}{\sqrt{N}} \quad \text{where } \overline{\overline{X}} \text{ is the "average average"}$$
$$= 45 + (3*19.1)/2.5$$
$$= 22.1 \text{ for the lower control limit.}$$

Thus, the average number of complaints for Hotel D is out of control because it falls outside these boundaries.

Exhibit 16-5. Control chart example.

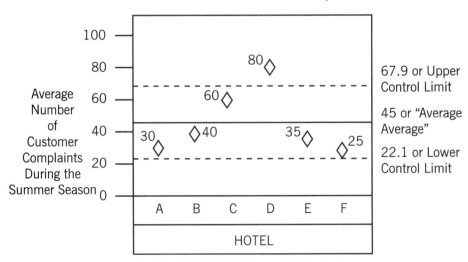

Trend charts track past performance and forecast results based on history. As shown in Exhibit 16-6, the chart shows the relationship between two variables. On the x-axis is a time span and on the y-axis is the value of a variable.

Using trend charts can be dangerous as well as useful. On the one hand, they require assuming that the future environment will be as in the past, thereby permitting forecasting. On the other hand, they enable long-range planning and playing "what-if" scenarios.

Analyze the Data

After compiling the data, Perry analyzes it. He reviews diagrams and looks at statistical compilations. Below is a table showing the compilation techniques employed and flags for assessing issues dealing with quality.

Compilation Technique	Flag
Pareto chart	Tallest bar indicates the largest "driver" for the cause of the problem.
Checksheets	Longest frequency of occurrences for a variable; thereby reflecting the focus of attention.
Scattergram	The most frequent occurrences and anomalies; the latter indicating a problem vis-à-vis normal behavior.
Control chart	Exceeding the upper control limit or going below the lower control limit, thereby indicating possible erratic, uncontrollable behavior of a process.
Trend chart	Upward or downward slope of the line, indicating a potential problem if the trend continues.

When analyzing the data, Perry will use several standard statistical calculations—specifically, mean, median, mode, and standard deviation. The *mean* is the average of the values for items in a group of data. The mean is best used when the original data are large enough not to be skewed by extreme values. The *median* is a position average at the midpoint for a frequency distribution. The median is best used when extreme values in the frequency distribution could distort the data. The *mode* is the value that appears most frequently in a series of numbers. The mode is used to avoid distortion by extreme values.

Standard deviation is another useful calculation. It determines the

Exhibit 16-6. Trend chart example.

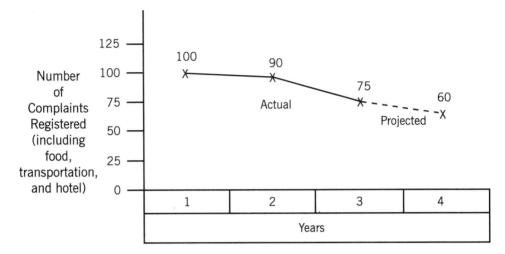

degree that each occurrence in a frequency distribution is located from the mean. In other words, it measures dispersion.

Exhibits 16-7 and 16-8 are examples of how to calculate the mean, median, mode, and standard deviation, respectively. In our example, the limousine service providing transportation for the Smythe wedding from the church to the reception wants to know the travel time between the two locations. The data they collected for five transportation times in minutes are shown below:

Column A Transportation Time in Minutes (or X)	Column B Average Time (or $\bar{X}$)	Column C $(X - \bar{X})$	Column D $(X - \bar{X})^2$
9	12	−3	9
10	12	−2	4
10	12	−2	4
12	12	0	0
19	12	7	49
Totals 60			66

Another quick, easy way to analyze data is to divide the data into quartiles, or four equal parts, after forming an array. The analyst counts down the array until he identifies the final item in the first 25 percent and then calculates up the array. Then he selects the midpoint between the end of the first and the top of the fourth quartile.

For example, on page 161 is a table of customer responses to a hotel

Fishbone Chart

Not all quality measurement tools are quantitative. The fishbone chart, also known as the Cause and Effect Diagram, is a diagramming method that identifies the cause of a problem by connecting four M's: *machines, manpower, materials,* and *methods.* At the end of the fishbone is a description of the effect of the problem. An example fishbone diagram is shown below:

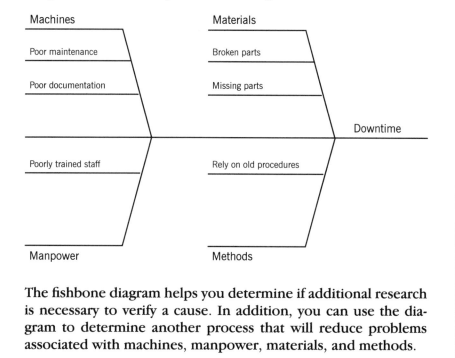

The fishbone diagram helps you determine if additional research is necessary to verify a cause. In addition, you can use the diagram to determine another process that will reduce problems associated with machines, manpower, materials, and methods.

survey of customer satisfaction. The hotel wants to know the results of their questionnaire, by quartiles. The calculation is shown in Exhibit 16-9.

Rating	Value	Number of Customer Responses	Quartile 1	Quartile 2	Quartile 3
Poor	1	5	5	5	5
Fair	2	0	0	0	0
Good	3	25	20 (of 25)	25	25
Very Good	4	30		20 (of 30)	30
Excellent	5	40			15 (of 40)
			25	50	75

Exhibit 16-7. Mean, median, and mode calculations.

Mean

The mean, or average, is calculated by summing the numbers from column A (60) and then dividing by the number of samples taken (also called *N*). The formula is:

Average time = sum of column A/*N*

$$= 60/5 = 12,$$ which is the average travel time between the two locations.

Median

The median is the middle number in a list of numbers. For our example, Perry arranges the numbers in column A from low to high: 9, 10, 10, 12, 19. The middle number of these five numbers is the third number, which is 10. Thus the median, or average, travel time between the two locations is 10.

Mode

The mode is the number occurring most frequently in a list of numbers. Again, Perry arranges the numbers in column A from low to high: 9, 10, 10, 12, 19. The number occurring most frequently is 10. Thus the mode, or average, travel time between the two locations is 10.

THE RESULTS OF DATA ANALYSIS

After converting his data into information and analyzing it, Perry will communicate the results. He does that in several ways, such as in a presentation or by sending e-mail. Whichever method he chooses, he states his assumptions—he does not hide them. For example, he might state that the information in the trend chart assumes that the project will proceed at the current pace.

Also, he portrays the data honestly and openly. He does not outlay charts or other information to cover up or skew the messages. Finally, he is consistent when collecting and reporting the information. Consistency ensures timely and useful information. Otherwise, he will have a credibility problem with the metrics.

SUMMING UP QUALITY ASSESSMENT

Collecting and analyzing metrics takes considerable time and effort. Perry knows, therefore, that it is imperative to define and get agreement upon what *quality* means, what metrics are necessary, and how to calculate them

Exhibit 16-8. Standard deviation calculation.

The standard deviation is defined as "how good the average is." In other words, how much it varies. An agent for the limousine service in the example of Exhibit 16-7 when asked the travel time between the church and reception locations might respond with "12 minutes on the average, give or take a few." The standard deviation answers how much that "few" is. The formula for the standard deviation is:

$$\text{Standard deviation} = \sqrt{\frac{\Sigma(X - \overline{X})^2}{N}}$$

where $(X - \overline{X})$ is the difference between column A and column B, and Σ means "the summation."

In column C, the differences are calculated and in column D they are squared and summed, yielding 66. According to the formula, 66 is then divided by N, or 5 for our example, which yields 13.2. Then Perry takes the square root of 13.2 to obtain 3.6, which is the standard deviation.

Thus, the average time of 12 minutes between the church and reception has a standard deviation of 3.2. This means that 68.27 percent of the time, Perry can expect it will take between 8.8 and 15.2 minutes for the trip (which is the mean of 12 minutes, plus or minus one standard deviation of 3.2 minutes; 12 − 3.2 = 8.8; 12 + 3.2 = 15.2).

For two standard deviations, or 95.45 percent of the time, Perry can expect it will take between 5.6 and 18.4 minutes for the trip (which is the mean of 12 minutes, plus or minus two standard deviations [or 3.2 × 2 = 6.4 minutes]; 12 − 6.4 = 5.6; 12 + 6.4 = 18.4.

Three standard deviations, or 99.73 percent of the time; following the same logic as above, it will take between 2.4 and 21.6 minutes for the trip.

---

prior to taking the first step. He then proceeds to implement metrics for the project, which in turn provide a baseline for managing change.

Questions for Getting Started

1. Do you know exactly what the customer's requirements are? If relevant, the internal customer? The external customer?
2. Is there an agreed-upon definition of what constitutes quality?
3. Did you get agreement on what to measure?
4. Did you get agreement on what metrics to use?

Exhibit 16-9. Quartile example.

From the table on page 161, Perry determines a quartile by taking the total number of customer responses (100) and dividing it into fourths. Thus, 100 divided by 4 equals 25. The following calculates the quartiles using the example in the table.

Perry now begins to calculate the first quartile. The "poor" rating contains five responses. The first quartile, however, is 25; therefore, he is 20 responses short (25 − 5). Thus, he must go to "fair," the next class, which has 0 responses. When 0 is added to 5, Perry is still 20 responses short of the first quartile. From the next higher class, "good," there are 25 responses; Perry needs 20 of those 25 to calculate the first quartile.

The formula for the first quartile is:

1 [from the "poor" rating] + 20/25 [from the "good" rating] = 1.8

Perry calculates the second quartile by taking the "first-half" of the responses, or 100 divided by 2, which equals 50. He now needs to add the 5 "poor" responses, 0 "fair" responses, 25 "good" responses," and 20 of the 30 "very good" responses to equal 50.

The formula for the second quartile is:

3 [the "good" rating] + 20/30 [from the "very good" rating] = 3.7

Perry calculates the third quartile by taking the first three-fourths of the responses, or three-fourths of 100, which equals 75 responses. He now needs to add the 5 "poor" responses, 0 "fair" responses, 25 "good" responses," 30 "very good" responses, and 15 of the 40 excellent responses to equal 75.

The formula for the third quartile is:

4 [the "very good" rating] + 15/40 [from the "excellent" rating] = 4.4

Hence, 25 percent of the respondents, or the first quartile, gave the hotel a rating of 1.8, which is approximately "fair." The second quartile, or 50 percent of the respondents, gave the hotel a rating of 3.7, which is almost "very good." This means that 50 percent of the customers gave the hotel a rating of "very good" or lower. For the third quartile, 75 percent of the respondents rated the hotel between "very good" and "excellent." This means that 75 percent of the customers gave the hotel a rating between "very good" and "excellent" or lower.

5. Have you identified what databases to use for metrics? Are the data reliable and valid?
6. Have you identified the expertise needed to perform the metrics? Is that expertise available? If not, how will you get that expertise?
7. Have you identified the hardware and software tools to do metrics? Are those tools available? If not, how will you get those tools?

8. How often do you plan to collect metrics?
9. Do you plan to use qualitative or quantitative metrics or both?
10. Are business considerations the major determinants of what metrics to use? If not, did you get buy-in to the metrics you plan to develop?
11. Have you identified your key process indicators (KBIs)?
12. For quantitative metrics, have you developed a formula? Did you get buy-in to the formula?
13. When using data for calculating metrics, did you cleanse the data? Standardize the data?
14. If developing Pareto charts, did you define the x- and y-axes? The flags to look for?
15. If using checksheets, did you determine the intervals to record each occurrence? Do you plan to display this information in the form of a histogram? The flags to look for?
16. If developing a histogram, did you define the x- and y-axes? The flags to look for?
17. If developing a control chart, did you identify the upper and lower control limits? The flags to look for?
18. If developing a trend chart, did you define the x- and y-axes? The flags to look for?
19. Do you need to calculate the mean? Median? Mode? Standard deviation? Quartile?
20. Do you have a plan for communicating the results?

Chapter 17

Managing Changes
to the Project

Ideally, Perry would like the Smythe Project to proceed as smoothly as possible—that is, according to plan. Yet he knows that nothing goes exactly according to plan. A project environment is dynamic, not static, and changes will have to be made.

MANAGING CHANGE

The key to handling project changes is to not resist them but to manage them. Perry puts in place good change management disciplines that will help him determine whether to implement contingency plans to deal with unanticipated events, take corrective action to get back on schedule, or make new plans for part of the project. Each action he will take significantly impacts project execution.

Managing change makes good practical sense. It helps Perry focus on the plan by identifying variances. It helps him maintain control by providing feedback on what is and should be happening at each step. Finally, it allows him the opportunity to adjust or modify plans so the goals remain realistic.

Of course, Perry knows that managing change is not easy. The project is constantly moving ahead, making it difficult to get an accurate snapshot. The right information in the right form at the right time is not readily available and in some cases is nonexistent. It takes time to develop and implement an infrastructure to detect, review, evaluate, and respond to changes. To deal with these obstacles and challenges, Perry must meet certain requirements.

1. He must have reliable, valid information. Bad data lead to bad information, which in turn can result in bad decisions.

2. He must have baselines to measure against. The baselines typically relate to cost, schedule, and quality. The baseline is the criterion against

which to judge actual performance. The variance is the difference between what is supposed to be and what is. Perry must make decisions regarding any variance. Those decisions might be to do nothing or to make changes.

3. He must have people who are adaptable to change. They should not be reactionaries or revolutionists, but realists. Presumably he has chosen such team members, but if not, he must determine how to deal with anyone who is overly resistant to change.

4. He must establish an infrastructure to manage change. He must institute policies, processes, and procedures for reviewing, analyzing, and responding to change. He must communicate these policies, processes, and procedures to team members. This infrastructure should also include people who are responsible for identifying, reviewing, analyzing, and responding to changes. If necessary, these people should help with scheduling, tracking, and monitoring the implementation of changes.

Perry will need to have a medium for capturing changes and tracking their fate, from identification to disposition. The medium, typically an electronic or hard copy form, is shown in Exhibit 17-1.

Exhibit 17-1. Approved request form.

Change Request Form
Instructions: Complete Part I of this form and retain the canary copy. Place the blue copy in the project library files. Submit the original to the project office. The project office will complete Part II and return a copy to you.
Part I—Completed by Requestor
Requestor Name: Smith, Patrick   Date: February 11, XX
Description of Change: Increase the number of invitations to the Smythe wedding by 20 percent; presume all parties invited will accept.
Impact of Change (who, what, when, where, and how): Perry Fitzberg to assign person to coordinate accordingly the increase in: catering and food services required; hotel accommodations; travel arrangements; transportation; and check for available seating in church and at reception.
Part II—Completed by Project Office
Category: Major _X_   Minor ___   Corrective ___
Priority: High _X_   Medium ___   Low ___
Approved: Yes _X_   No ___   Deferred ___   Date Completed: March 10, XX

Decision-Making Basics

As a project manager, you will make decisions throughout a project. The hardest decisions with the most risk come during latter phases, when the time is less and the impact more acute. Remember the following basics of decision making.

1. Know when a decision is required. Be able to look at circumstances and determine if a decision is necessary. Usually an anomaly or variance to a plan signals the need for a decision.

2. Determine your objectives. In other words, the decision must be purposeful.

3. Develop several alternatives. Brainstorm either by yourself or with team members.

4. Select the alternative that promises to provide the greatest payoff. How do you determine which alternative that is? By developing a method, such as a weighted point scheme, to evaluate how well each alternative satisfies the objectives. Then you rank the alternatives by score. The alternative with the highest score is the one you select.

5. Develop and implement a plan. Since a project manager rarely has command and control over team members, get buy-in for your plan.

6. Seek feedback while implementing the plan. This feedback will help you to refine the plan and indicate how well you are achieving the objectives.

Types of Changes

To identify whether a change is necessary, Perry establishes a series of baselines. Baselines are agreed-upon points of reference. In the project environment, baselines are set for schedule, budget, and quality.

Ideally, a project proceeds according to its baselines. However, variances can occur, and the project manager must decide how to respond to those variances. First, however, the project manager analyzes and evaluates the nature of a change. Many changes are internal, such as adjusting how a task is done because of an unrealistic specification. Other changes originate from external sources. The customer or senior management may, for example, arbitrarily reduce funding or change scope.

Perry develops a classification scheme for such changes. He classifies them as major, minor, or corrective.

- A *major* change dramatically affects schedule, cost, or quality. Examples include across-the-board cuts in budget, expansion of the scope of the project without increasing the budget, or acceleration of the scheduled completion date.
- A *minor* change is one that does not fit in the major category. Examples include a small change in the specifications or requirements.
- A *corrective* change is nice to have but unnecessary. An example might be addressing an overlooked "nice-to-have" specification.

Whether major, minor, or corrective, Perry assigns each change a priority. A priority can be either major, minor, or deferral.

- A *high priority* change demands immediate attention. It is a "show stopper." Generally, such changes are major changes, too, but not necessarily. The customer, for example, would like to significantly change the specifications, but the change is not doable without substantial changes to the schedule, budget, or quality of the desired result.
- A *medium priority* change does not require immediate attention. However, it must be addressed before the project ends. An example is an important but small change to the specifications.
- A *low priority* change is addressed, if time permits. These changes include "nice-to-have" features or offers in a product or service, respectively.

Perry, of course, does not alone make decisions or change categories and priorities. He forms a change board, which consists of people responsible for classifying and prioritizing changes. The people on the change board are typically the project manager, selected team members, and customer representatives.

The change board does more, however, than just categorize and prioritize changes. It also analyzes the impact of such changes on cost, schedule, and quality. It approves or disapproves the changes, and it assigns responsibilities for executing these changes.

Corrective Action

Sometimes the contingency plans do not work or an unanticipated event occurs. Either case, it impacts cost, schedule, and quality and requires corrective action. This means taking steps to get the project back on track.

To take corrective action, Perry must address some challenges.

1. He must have sufficient data to define the problem and determine a solution.

2. He must distinguish between causes and symptoms. Using good analytical techniques can help, but so will good data, especially if it answers the who, what, when, where, why, and how of the situation.

3. He must respond quickly. Procrastination and indecisiveness can convert a problem into a crisis.

4. He must recognize that corrective action occurs throughout the project cycle. There is a tendency for project managers to think that everything is fine up front, only to be surprised toward the end that corrective action should have been taken earlier.

5. He must seek feedback on the corrective action taken. The feedback should indicate whether the problem disappeared.

REPLANNING

If corrective actions are inadequate, Perry knows the next step: replanning. Replanning is redoing the project plan by making wholesale changes to cost, schedule, and quality factors.

There are several reasons for replanning. First, it makes more sense to follow a realistic plan. Likewise, the team works more efficiently because the changes have reduced confusion. The team is also more effective in achieving the project goal.

To replan well, Perry must address certain prerequisites.

1. He must have reliable and valid data to determine whether replanning is necessary.

2. He must act quickly. If not, replanning will break synergy. It will also detract from productivity, even under the old plan.

3. He and everyone else must have patience. Replanning takes effort and diagnosing past performance can be sensitive. Some people do not want to replan; it only adds frustration. Other people fear being blamed for the circumstances that led to the replanning.

4. He does replanning as early as possible. During the early phases of a project, replanning is easier. Many unknowns are expected and the momentum is just beginning. However, it is more difficult to replan during the latter phases. The momentum is faster, people are rushing to accomplish major milestones, and it becomes more costly to do any rework.

5. He understands the impact that replanning will have. Will the replanning be expensive? How much time and other resources will be required to replan? When must replanning be complete? What impact will replanning have on cost, schedule, and quality?

When replanning, Perry remembers that there is no such thing as a free lunch. If he decides to schedule, there will be negative and positive effects. The same can be said for cost, quality, and people factors.

Problem Solving

Life is full of problems, and projects have their share. These problems can overwhelm the best project managers. It is important, therefore, to approach identifying and solving problems systematically.

Here are some rudimentary steps for solving problems.

1. Define the situation. That is, determine the variables or factors that indicate whether a problem exists. Sliding of tasks on the critical path is an example.

2. Keep your cool. Do not let your emotions rule you and do not jump to conclusions. Focus on defining the problem, answering the who, what, when, where, why, and how.

3. Do not confuse symptoms with causes. It is easy to misdiagnose the problem by focusing on a symptom. Look at the big picture and then narrow to the issue. Define the problem in one or two sentences.

4. Keep personality out of the picture. Liking or disliking someone usually has nothing to do with a problem; failure to recognize that fact can cloud your objectivity in developing a meaningful solution.

5. Develop a plan. Devise a miniature project plan, if you will, to implement a solution.

6. Seek feedback. You may have addressed the cause but perhaps not in a way that completely fixes the problem. Feedback will help you to refine your plan and achieve your solution.

Perry, for instance, decides to change the logic of the network diagram because the Smythe family wants to have the bridal shower two weeks earlier. The Smythe family also wants to increase the number of attendees by 20 percent and add more events. All this affects the schedule, of course, but also the scope of the project. The changes also have positive and negative impacts. A positive impact is satisfying the customer; a negative impact is temporarily slowing the momentum of the project, which in turn reduces productivity.

CONTINGENCY PLANNING

Ideally, risk assessment (see Chapter 12) provides the basis for good contingency planning. Contingency planning involves developing responses

Exhibit 17-2. Contingency plan form.

Contingency Plan Form

Instructions: Complete this form and file a copy in the project history file
and the project manual.

Preparer: <u>Perry Fitzberg</u>   Date: <u>February 21, XXXX</u>

Description of Event: <u>Additional guests invited to Smythe wedding (increase by</u>
<u>20 percent).</u>

Description of Impact to Cost, Schedule, and Quality:
<u>Cost rises including: food and catering; and transportation to church and</u>
<u>reception</u>

<u>Schedule may be impacted including: availability of additional food, vehicles,</u>
<u>and accommodations—may need to outsource if necessary</u>

<u>Quality may be degraded including: quality of service, food, travel/transporta-</u>
<u>tion, and accommodations due to availability</u>

Probability of Occurrence: High <u>X</u>   Medium ___   Low ___

Description of Planned Response: <u>Communicate to caterers, transportation ser-</u>
<u>vices, hotels, and the church the need for an increase from the original</u>
<u>request. Have them detail their plans for delivery to meet the revised</u>
<u>Smythe requiremens.</u>

---

to situations that have a good probability of occurrence and could impact
project performance.

For the Smythe Project, Perry develops a contingency form, shown in
Exhibit 17-2. He records the description of the event; its probability of
occurrence; its impact on cost, schedule, and quality; and the appropriate
response.

Reliable contingency plans don't just happen, as Perry well knows.
They require having information about possible events, including their potential impact; time preparation; and feedback indicating when the events
do occur.

Summing Up Change Management

The project environment is not static. No matter what plans or baseline he
establishes, Perry knows that he will have to evaluate and implement

changes. He also knows that change affects costs, schedule, quality, or a combination of them. He is determined to manage change; otherwise, change will manage him and he can quickly lose control.

Questions for Getting Started

1. If you decided to take corrective action, did you:
   - Determine exactly what caused the need for corrective action?
   - Determine the most appropriate corrective action and implement it?
   - Receive input from the people affected by the corrective action?
   - Set a "blockpoint" date for the corrective action to be implemented?
   - Communicate the corrective action in advance?
   - Seek feedback after the corrective action was implemented?
2. If replanning, did you:
   - Determine what is the cause for replanning?
   - Determine what areas (e.g., cost, schedule, quality) of the project are affected by the replanning? The negative and positive impacts?
   - Determine resource requirements and their availability for resource planning?
   - Determine the data and information requirements for replanning?
   - Obtain input from all of the people affected by the replanning?
   - Obtain feedback from all the affected people once the new plans went into effect?
3. If doing contingency planning, did you:
   - Determine and document the possible events using the risk assessment?
   - For each event, determine and document the probability of occurrence, the projected impact, and the appropriate response?
   - Make sure the plans are readily available?
   - Assign someone responsible for upkeeping and executing the contingency plan?
   - Receive input from the people affected by the contingency plan?
   - Obtain and assess relevant feedback from the individuals affected by the contingency plan after it has been implemented?

4. Did you establish a change management infrastructure that includes a means for:
    - Classifying changes?
    - Prioritizing changes?
    - Evaluating changes (e.g., change board)?
    - Documenting changes?
    - Tracking, monitoring, and addressing changes?
    - Communicating changes?
    - Following up on changes?

Chapter 18
Project Closure

All projects eventually end. Some end successfully, others end in disasters. Some common reasons why projects end poorly are changing market conditions, lack of cooperation from clients, lack of management support, lack of resources, politics, technical problems, and poor management. Exhibit 18-1 sums up the management reasons for failure, while Exhibit 18-2 lists reasons for success.

Fortunately for Perry, the Smythe Project ended successfully: the wedding proceeded as planned, meeting all milestone dates on time, consuming all monies within the budgeted amount, and giving the Smythe family exactly what they wanted. Unlike other weddings, the team's morale was extremely high up to the very end.

Despite overwhelming success, not everything worked perfectly. Some communications, coordination, and implementation problems

Exhibit 18-1. Common reasons for project failure.

Leading
- Avoiding conflict
- Burning out of team members
- Delaying decision making
- Lacking cooperation
- Lacking customer involvement
- Lacking senior management support
- Communicating poorly
- Setting unrealistic expectations

Defining
- Having ill-defined, too large, too small a scope
- Having incomplete or unclear requirements

Planning
- No planning
- Poorly formulating plans
- Having unclear, unrealistic plans

Organizing
- Lacking resources
- Lacking accurate knowledge and expertise
- Having unclear authorities and responsibilities

Controlling
- Failing to deal with a changing environment
- Failing to manage change
- Overemphasizing on technology issues at expense of business issues
- Competing too much for resources

Closure
- Finding errors too late
- Failing to learn from past problems

Exhibit 18-2. Common reasons for project success.

Leading
- Having the support of senior management
- Obtaining customer involvement
- Maintaining realistic expectations
- Encouraging and sustaining a sense of owner-ship by all participants
- Having commitment and cooperation of all participants
- Promoting integrity

Organizing
- Assigning responsibility for well-defined deliv-erables
- Having a good communication infrastructure in place
- Having clear lines of authorities and responsi-bilities
- Having a team with requisite knowledge and expertise

Defining
- Chunking the project into manageable pieces
- Keep the scope well-defined
- Clear definition of requirements
- Focus on customer
- Clear mission and objectives

Controlling
- Having a documented change management in place
- Holding regular and frequent meetings
- Avoiding scope "creep"
- Taking regular measurements of performance

Planning
- Focusing evenly on technical and business issues
- Developing meaningful plans
- Having more frequent project milestones
- Having shorter flow time
- Simplifying

Closure
- Releasing people correctly to minimize impact on morale and performance

arose, and projects Perry handles in the future will benefit from what he learned.

LEARNING FROM PAST EXPERIENCE

Perry collects and compiles statistics from the project by using the project data repository. Mainly the measurements used during the project, these data help Perry ascertain what did and did not go well. He plans to include the information in a special document.

The *lessons-learned document* captures the successes, challenges, and other information of a project. Managers of similar projects in the future can refer to what is in the document and, consequently, operate more efficiently and effectively. The lessons-learned document not only communicates useful information to future project managers, but also helps to identify their own strengths and weaknesses. But these advantages can be realized only if the document is well prepared. The outline for a lessons-learned document is shown in Exhibit 18-3. Many times, the document is poorly written, contains unsubstantiated claims and personal

Exhibit 18-3. Outline for a lessons-learned document.

Lessons-Learned Document

I.   Present title page, which includes:
   A. Document title
   B. Document number
   C. Original release date
   D. Appropriate signatures and date

II.   Present table of contents, which includes:
   A. Section headings
   B. Relevant page numbers

III.   Present introduction, which includes:
   A. Goals
   B. Scope
   C. Objectives, like
      ▪ Technical
      ▪ Business
   D. History/background information

IV. Present events, and what went right; what went wrong, and what was done; and what might have been done otherwise, which include:
   A. Activities
   B. Critical items
   C. Major milestone deliverables
   D. Political actions
   E. Roadblocks

V.   Present summary, which includes a wrap-up of the project

grandstanding, and is filed in an inaccessible place. To ensure that these shortcomings do not appear, Perry takes the following actions.

1. He ensures that the data are useful. This task is easy since he has collected reliable, valid measures throughout the project.

2. He identifies other sources of information. Since he collected and organized data throughout the project, this action is easy. He especially uses the information in the project history files.

3. He assigns someone on the noncritical path to do the preliminary work for preparing the document. This includes collecting documents and data, as well as preparing the draft. This approach allows Perry to handle concurrent activities during project closure.

Information Systems Projects: A Lesson for Everyone

Although project failure appears in all industries, information systems (IS) projects seem to get special attention. Their record of successes and failures has been referred to by some as a crapshoot.

It's no surprise. The news is replete with examples of IS projects having disastrous results. The state of Washington stopped developing a system that would process driver's licenses and vehicle registration; the project was several years behind schedule and millions of dollars over budget. California had even more disastrous results while developing a large PC-based network—the project was millions of dollars over budget and lasted over twelve years. And as with Washington, California had a Department of Motor Vehicles project that blew its schedule and exceeded its budget. Then there is the Oregon Driver and Motor Vehicle Services project, which has exceeded twice its original cost estimate.

Do not blame the public sector, however. The private sector has had its share of failures. The Xerox IS project, called the Market to Collection Project, passed its scheduled completion date by two years and exceeded its budget.

These examples may be more common than first realized. In the late 1980s, Capers Jones, president of Software Productivity Research, revealed some sobering statistics about projects with more than 64,000 lines of code. He noted that less than 1 percent finished on time, within budget, and met all user requirements. The "average" project was more than a year late and the cost was double the estimate.[1] Almost seven years later, the Standish Group announced that IS development projects succeed only slightly more than 1 percent—that is, finishing on time and within budget. If an organization is large, the success rate drops.[2]

What are the major contributors to such dismal results? According to the Center for Project management, 73 percent of the companies it surveyed had inadequately defined project plans. Less than 25 percent had well-defined and practical project management processes.[3]

1. "Software Productivity and Quality," *System Development*, April 1987, pp. 1–6.
2. "Few IS Projects Come in On Time, On Budget," *Computerworld*, December 12, 1994.
3. "Pesky Projects," *Computerworld*, April 11, 1994, p. 118.

4. He solicits input from project participants for ideas and information to include in the document. This ensures a more objective and complete document. He has team members review the draft to preclude any biased content.

5. He submits the document to senior management, whose responsibility is to ensure that it is not forgotten and apply its contents to similar projects in the future.

RELEASING PEOPLE AND EQUIPMENT

At closure, Perry must release the people who have worked on the project. Releasing people is not simple. If released inefficiently and ineffectively, morale problems can occur. If there's a feeling of pending disaster, people may depart prematurely and leave tasks unfinished.

Since it is a matrix environment, Perry knows that prematurely releasing people may mean losing them permanently. So he reviews the responsibility matrices and schedule to determine the remaining work. He then releases only those without work, since people sitting idle will in time interfere with the others' productivity, spread rumors, or add unnecessary labor costs. Perry also ceases use of any unnecessary equipment or facilities.

RECOGNIZING AND REWARDING PEOPLE

No project is complete without recognition for outstanding performance. While conceptually simple, Perry knows in reality its implementation is difficult. He must decide whether to reward individuals or the team or both, what the most meaningful recognitions would be, and what rewards are within his power. These are difficult to determine; still Perry follows some basic principles when giving recognition and rewards.

1. He strives for objectivity. He uses objective criteria for measuring results. It is hard to forget the past or divorce yourself from the personalities of the individuals. The only way to avoid those circumstances is to be as objective as possible.

2. He determines the values and behaviors he wants to reward. He rewards these values and behaviors that best satisfy those of the company.

3. He remembers the expectancy theory. Expectancy theory states that successful performance depends on people's expectations of rewards, whether extrinsic or intrinsic. In other words, a person's expenditure of effort depends on his or her expectations of reward. If a person expects a

financial reward and receives a nonfinancial one, morale might fall and productivity decline.

4. He appears fair and consistent. If several people gave outstanding performances, he gives them equal recognition and rewards. Even the appearance of being unfair or inconsistent can cheapen a recognition or reward.

5. He is timely. He presents the recognitions and rewards within a reasonable time to gain maximum motivational value. If he gives recognitions or rewards long after completing a milestone, for example, they lose their meaning and impact.

6. He does not rely on monetary rewards. In fact, he avoids them. Money provides only short-term satisfaction and can prove divisive, especially if a person feels shortchanged. He uses a variety of nonfinancial rewards, from plaques to dinners to trips. For many project managers in a matrix environment, such rewards may be all they are entitled to dispense.

Some Guidelines for Future Projects

Throughout the project, Perry kept a balance between the classical and the behavioral aspects of the project. He knew that a detailed work structure or formal change control procedures are simply tools for completing his project. In other words, they are the means to an end, not the end themselves. Using these tools requires good judgment; therefore he was continually asking himself: Did the statement of work give a real portrayal of what had to be done? Was the planning sufficient and could I have anticipated problems better? What procedural changes would I make next time?

These are tough questions and often there are no definitive answers. Project managers must use their judgment, which is based on their knowledge, experience, and expertise. Nevertheless, there are some general guidelines that are useful for making good judgments.

1. The costlier the project, the more important it is that project management disciplines be in place. A large monetary investment indicates a project's level of importance—for example, a $1 million project is more important than a $10,000 one. It makes sense, therefore, that the monies for the larger project are all accounted for and justifiable. Project management disciplines help ensure that inefficiencies do not occur.

2. The larger the project team, the more important it is that project management be used. Larger project teams present greater challenges for coordination and communication. For example, a fifty-person project is more difficult to coordinate than a five-person one.

3. The greater the complexity of the final product, the more important it is that management disciplines are in place. For example, building a state-of-the-art information system is more complex than building an outdoor shed. The former requires greater coordination of personnel and resources.

4. The longer the project, the more important it is that all procedures and schedules be in place. Along with more time to complete a project is the tendency to overlook the need for good project management. The "we'll do it later" syndrome takes over and often results in key elements never being implemented or implemented in a mad rush at the last minute. The project managers should identify and implement as many elements as early as possible, before the project gains too much momentum.

5. The more ambiguity there is about a project's scope, the more discipline needs to be imposed on the project. The project manager must define the goal of the project and develop a path for achieving it. If the project lacks clarity of purpose, then coordination, communication, and other key activities become difficult, even impossible.

6. A lack of precedence requires that more discipline be in place. If a project of a similar nature has never been done, then there's a greater likelihood that management may be stymied. For example, previous experience leads the way to greater efficiency and effectiveness.

7. The more dynamic the project environment, the more procedures and schedules should be in place. If the environment is constantly in flux, then the project must be adaptable to change yet retain the focus on the goal. Project management tools help achieve focus and adaptability by evaluating the impact of changes as they appear.

The six functions of project management are critical to success; however the degree of application remains a matter of judgment. These guidelines can help the project manager decide what tools and techniques should be applied and to what degree. In the end, however, the project manager makes the decisions regarding management of his or her project.

Questions for Getting Started

1. If collecting and compiling statistics, did you:
   - Determine all the sources of information?
   - Decide whether the data are reliable and valid?
   - Determine what is required to make the data meaningful (if it is not)?
2. If preparing a lessons learned document, did you:
   - Determine all the sources of information?
   - Prepare an outline?

- Take steps to ensure its objectivity?
- Submit it to senior management or other people who might use the information in the future?

3. When releasing people, did you determine the criteria to identify who should remain and who should be redeployed?

4. When releasing equipment, facilities, etc., did you determine the criteria to identify what should remain and what should be redeployed?

5. When recognizing and rewarding people, did you:
   - Determine whether to reward the entire team or select individuals or both?
   - Seek to be objective?
   - Appear fair and consistent?
   - Determine what recognition and rewards approaches are available to you?
   - Match the expectancy of recognition and reward with the type sought by the team or individuals?

Part III
Project Management Enhancement

Chapter 19

Automated Project Management

Project management software can help you generate a project plan quickly, produce reports rapidly and consistently, perform "what if" scenarios, identify inconsistencies with data, and reuse data from similar projects. In short, today's software can go quite far in helping project managers be more effective in their job.

Using project management software, despite its obvious benefits, presents some challenges, too. Some of these challenges include getting people to understand the purpose of the programs; reducing the learning curve; increasing people's receptivity to the output; producing reliable information rather than garbage in, garbage out; and ensuring that the software program supports the project and not that the project supports the software. Of course, you must also have the right hardware, operating software, and utilities on hand; the software must be available at a reasonable price; and the licensing agreements must be fair.

You can use project management software to calculate early and late dates for each task and to determine the critical path. You also can use software to allocate resources and calculate costs. In addition, you can use word processing software to draft the statement of work and a spreadsheet program to estimate the hours needed to complete the project.

Today, automated project management is going through immense changes. In the past, the scope was fairly narrow; software was used to build schedules and calculate costs. But the advent of local area networks, Web technologies, and mobile computing have expanded the scope of automated project management dramatically. Current—and future—applications will drastically change the way projects are completed and help ensure their completion on time and within budget.

The discussion in this chapter visualizes the structure of present-day automated project management in the form of a three-level pyramid, as shown in Exhibit 19-1.

Exhibit 19-1. Automated project management structure.

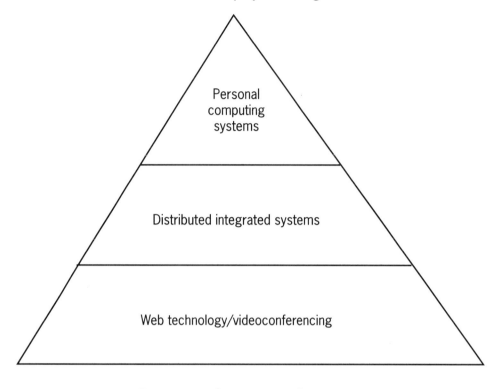

Personal Computing Systems

Building a program plan and doing risk assessment requires an automated project management package, easiest on a personal computer. There are software packages at the minicomputer or mainframe level, but their purchase or lease costs often are too high, the number of records insufficient, and the learning curve too long for most limited-term projects. PC packages have the capabilities of larger systems but can be used at PC level.

To choose a software package, consider your needs. A project manager might likely have the following requirements:

Typical Software Needs and Wants

- Cover a large number of tasks.
- Assign multiple resources to a task and generate resource histograms for each resource and composite ones.
- Build a project repository.
- Choose different types of network diagrams that provide multiple displays of information.
- Create bar charts for multiple levels of the work breakdown structure and have the ability to tailor and custom-build.

What the Software Won't Do

Many project managers, especially inexperienced ones, believe that the software makes or breaks a project. Unfortunately, this belief is as unrealistic as the idea that a paintbrush makes a good painter or a pencil makes a good writer.

Software is simply a tool to help you manage a project. It is an aid, an enabler—if you use it correctly. It will help you make decisions. It will help you communicate with people. It will help you track performance and take corrective action, if necessary.

The software, however, will not do these things for you. You must make the decisions. You must communicate. You must take action to get back on track. In other words, you must provide the leadership to bring a project in on time and within budget. It happens because of you, not because of the software.

Many project managers have a tendency to blame the tool when things go awry. That serves only as an excuse for poor project management. After all, as an old saying goes, good carpenters never blame their tools.

If this sounds like preaching, it is, and heed the warning. Many a project has failed despite the availability and use of the best project management software tools.

- Define and change the logic relationships between tasks as well as the lag value for all network diagrams.
- Detect logic errors in network diagrams and identify the problem.
- Establish a baseline, or target, schedule to measure against.
- Generate graphics (e.g., pie charts and Pareto diagrams) using data from the repository.
- Offer a common user interface that enables using other application packages easily.
- Perform "automatic" resource leveling.
- Perform "what if" scenarios to determine the impact of the cost and schedule milestones.
- Provide calendaring capabilities that can be modified to suit specific circumstances.
- Provide standardized reports and have ability to tailor and custom-build.
- Use with other well-known word processing, database, and spreadsheet programs.

Assign a value to each software need to reflect its relative priority, as shown in Exhibit 19-2. Then collect literature (e.g., sales brochures and magazine

Exhibit 19-2. Sample software evaluation.

Requirements	Weight	Package A		Package B		Package C	
		Value	Calculated (Weight × Value)	Value	Calculated (Weight × Value)	Value	Calculated (Weight × Value)
Build a project repository	3	2	6 (3 × 2)	3	9 (3 × 3)	1	3 (3 × 1)
Add level number of tasks	2	3	6	3	6	2	4
Select different types of network diagrams	1	2	2	2	2	1	1
Provide standardized reports and ability to modify each one	3	1	3	1	3	3	9
Establish baseline schedule	3	2	6	1	3	3	9
Create and tailor bar charts	1	1	1	2	2	3	3
Define and change logic relationships	2	1	2	3	6	2	4
Assign multiple resources to tasks	3	1	3	2	6	1	3
Perform automatic resource leveling	3	1	3	3	9	3	9
Grand Total			32		46		45

reviews), experiment with demos to see how well they satisfy your needs, and interview subject matter experts. Finally, tally the results of your investigation and select the best package based on the total score.

Remember that selecting the right package involves more than performing mechanical steps.

1. The agreement. Should you buy individual packages or multiple packages? If the latter, will you receive a discount?

2. How easy is it to learn the package? Will the vendor provide basic training?

3. What type of support services are there? Is there a support line? Is there a charge for consultation? Is it available 7 by 24, meaning seven days a week, twenty-four hours a day?

4. How long has the vendor been in business? If not long, what happens if it goes out of business after you have invested in its product?

5. How well can the package be integrated with other popular applications and other projects (e.g., spreadsheets)? Will it require complex programming to share data?

6. How long is the learning curve? Will it help the team focus on the work rather than on satisfying the needs of the software? In other words, is the software an enabler?

Once the package is selected and delivered, ensure that team members understand how to use the software and provide the output. The need and level of understanding depends on the audience, of course. People working directly on the project team (e.g., core team members) need a more detailed understanding of the capabilities and outputs than senior management and the customer. Hence, tailor your presentation to reflect these different needs.

Follow the same process when selecting risk management software. Identify the needs and wants in the software package, find several popular packages, apply an objective approach to select the right software, and ensure that people using the software are trained sufficiently. Some leading project management and risk management software packages are shown in Exhibits 19-3 and 19-4.

Distributed Integrated System

Although there are excellent packages for project management, more often than not the computing environment is distributed, whereby processing power is split among different levels in a systems architecture. A distributed computing architecture is client/server. That is, some or all the application processing may reside at the client, or PC, level, or be shared with a server, or be at a mini- or mainframe computer level.

A typical scenario is for the project application software to reside on the client; the major processing and data occur on the server. This architecture offers several advantages. First, users have a user-friendly interface while simultaneously having access to considerably more power and data than on a PC. Second, hardware and software cost less since the preliminary work is done at the client level. And third, data can be shared among multiple users as well as provide uniform data management.

The client/server environment has substantially affected project management as a complementary or supplementary tool for new technologies such as telecommuting, mobile computing, and groupware.

Telecommuting

Increasingly, people work on projects via personal computers in their homes. They provide their services and expertise electronically. Telecom-

---

Project Management Methodologies

In some situations, projects can make use of a project management methodology, or PMM. Sometimes the methodology is developed in-house; other times it is purchased from an outside firm. Whatever its origins, a PMM offers several advantages. It provides a consistent, standardized approach for managing projects. It sets the groundwork for compiling data. And it improves communications.

The PMM must be flexible in its application. It must also be documented and accessible, and it should be supported via training and vendor assistance. Finally, it should present information clearly and concisely.

A PMM does not guarantee success; it takes leadership to get people to use the PMM. And this leadership should come not from just the project manager but also from senior management. Commitment comes just as much from the top as it does from the rank and file.

Some PMMs are stand-alone, meaning they're not part of a much bigger methodology—for example, the Practical Project Management Methodology (P^2M^2) by Practical Creative Solutions and KLR Consulting. Other PMMs are part of a much bigger methodology, such as Productivity Plus ($P+$) by DMR, which is oriented toward software development.

---

muting reduces the need for office space, plus saves time and commuting dollars for the individual. It allows people to accomplish more in less time, thanks to fewer interruptions and a flexible work schedule.

There are challenges to telecommuting, and many of them are financial. Telecommuters must have technological tools, including a personal computer (e.g., laptop or workstation), software (e.g., terminal emulation), modem, printer, pager, and cellular phone. They also need training and perhaps technical support to resolve connections problems and answer advanced application quieries. Project managers must ensure that telecommuters have the current software, from project management to word processing.

There are also potential performance problems. There is corruption and other degradations of data associated with transferring data across telephone lines. Slow transmission speed can increase costs, requiring installation of high bandwidth lines.

Exhibit 19-3. Leading project management software packages.

Package	Description	Contact
Primavera Project Planner (copyright)	A comprehensive planning and control package. It also provides e-mail and Web publishing functionality. Considered useful for medium to large projects.	Primavera Systems, Inc. Two Bala Plaza Bala Cynwyd, PA 19004-1586 (610) 667-8600 www.primavera.com
Results Management	A suite of project management products, of which Project Workbench plays a key role. Project Workbench provides an extensive project planning and control system. Considered useful for medium to large projects.	ABT Corporation 361 Broadway New York, NY 10013-3998 (212) 219-8945 www.abtcorp.com
Microsoft Project for Windows	A planning and controlling package that generates standard and tailorable charts and reports. Microsoft Project for Windows works well with other Microsoft products. Considered useful for small to medium projects.	Microsoft Corporation One Microsoft Way Redmond, WA 98052-6399 (425) 635-7155 www.msn.com
CA-Superproject	A project management package that is very resource driven and provides extensive graphics and reporting capabilities. Considered useful for small to large projects.	Computer Associates International, Inc. One Computer Associates Plaza Islandia, NY 11788-7000 (800) 225-5224 www.cai.com
Project Scheduler 7 for Windows	A project management package noted for ease of use, resource handling capabilities, and managing multiple projects. Considered useful for small to large projects.	Scitor Corporation 333 Middlefield Road 2nd floor Menlo Park, CA 94025 (800) 533-9876 www.scitor.com

Mobile Computing

Like telecommuting, mobile computing is a result of advances in client/server technology. Project team members can be on the road and still contribute to deliverables. It gives team members the flexibility to work at different locations, and enables them to work at a remote location and still provide timely results.

Exhibit 19-4. Leading risk management software packages.

Package	Description	Contact
Monte Carlo for Primavera	Risk analysis software that is used with Primavera Project Planner. It enables determining the probabilities for completing a project on schedule and within budget.	Primavera Systems, Inc. Two Bala Plaza Bala Cynwyd, PA 19004-1586 (610) 667-8600 www.primavera.com
Rank-It	Risk assessment software that enables applying precedence diagramming (not to be confused with precedence network diagramming for schedules) for identifying and ranking threats and processes and associated controls.	Jerry Fitzgerald and Associates 506 Barkentine Lane Redwood City, CA 94065-1128 (415) 591-5676 //ourworld.compuserve.com/homepages/jerardra
Risk +	Risk analysis software to use with Microsoft Project for Windows. It enables applying Monte Carlo simulation to determine the probability to complete tasks.	Program Management Solutions, Inc. 553 N. Pacific Coast Highway Suite B-177 Redondo Beach, CA 90278 (805) 898-9571 www.prog-mgmt.com
Total Risk	An integrated risk management package for monitoring and controlling risk by creating a "virtual data warehouse."	Redpoint Software, Inc. One Cabot Road Suite 190 Hudson, MA 01749 (508) 870-0070 www.rpsi.com

Of course, there are challenges to mobile computing. The costs can be high. A mobile computing workforce requires laptops, batteries, printers, software (e.g., applications, communications), CD-ROM attachments, modems, adapters, docking stations, PCMCIA cards, and drivers.

There are other factors, too: skyrocketing communications costs, additional servers to handle demand, training, and support to resolve technical problems. And there is the time and money to ensure the data security and restrictive access to corporate networks.

Groupware Computing

Thanks to client/server architecture and the movement toward flatter organizational structures, groupware computing enables the sharing of applications and data. Groupware is often not enterprise-wide; it is used within a smaller organization, such as a department, work unit, or project. Its software components fall into one of these categories:

- Electronic mail and messaging over a network
- Information sharing (e.g., document management)
- Personal and group calendaring and scheduling
- Real-time conferencing (e.g., electronic meetings)
- Workflow (e.g., automation of common business functions)

To function in a groupware environment, team members need microcomputers or workstations, servers, cabling, network devices, and software (which often includes two or more categories). It requires a commonality of software and data.

Groupware improves the communciation and distribution of information. It capitalizes on trends toward decentralization of computing, using mid-range and personal computer-based computing. But groupware also presents its challenges. Like telecommuting and mobile computing, it requires support personnel to resolve technical difficulties and answer inquiries. There must be a substantial initial investment in hardware and software, as well as upgrade efforts and training. All this increases project costs and adds to flow time.

Web Technology

The Internet is revolutionary technology that ties organizations and projects together. Many companies apply Web technology in the form of *intranets.* The broad, primary difference between the Internet and an intranet is that the latter uses a firewall, or server, to regulate or screen communications—hence, Internet technology is used on a smaller, restricted basis.

The technology for using the Internet or an intranet is varied, but they share common requirements:

- Workstation and browser for each user
- Database servers
- Expertise in SQL (structured query language), HTML (hypertext markup language), CGI (common gateway interface), Java, and a database management system (e.g., relational)
- Operating system at the workstation
- Protocols (such as HTTP, TCP/IP) for communications

Web technology is truly an enabler of projects. It gives people access to information that was once difficult to obtain. It has tools (browsers, HTML [hypertext markup language], etc.) that are relatively easy to use and piggyback on an existing communications network and client/server infrastructures. Finally, it furthers communication through e-mail or conferencing at relatively low cost.

Web Site Design

The enthusiasm for Web technology has hit just about every organization. Even medium-size projects are building their own Web sites. Quite often, the Web pages of these sites appear cluttered, confusing, and irrelevant.

To develop a Web page for your project, ensure that it is clear, concise, consistent, relevant, and simple. Your Web pages should:

- Follow a logical structure rather than appear as a hodge-podge of unrelated data.
- Have text free of spelling and grammatical errors.
- Keep hypertext and navigational links to a minimum and current.
- Use color sparingly to emphasize main points and draw attention.
- Use graphics, audio, and video to support the main focus of the site, not distract.
- Use language that is familiar to everyone; define acronyms and jargon.
- Use plenty of white space to increase readability and minimize bandwidth use.

Many projects establish Web sites. A Web site is what people inside and outside of the project access to send or obtain information.

A project typically has one Web site for people access, which provides hypertext links to contents throughout the site and navigational links to other pertinent sites. The information likely to be on a Web site is:

- Cost and time estimates
- Forms
- Lessons learned from previous projects
- Meeting schedules
- Memorandums
- Phone and contact listings
- Procedures
- Reports
- Risk assessment
- Schedules (bar and network)
- Statement of work
- Work breakdown structure

Taming the E-Mail Beast

In the past, it was not uncommon for project managers to find a pile of memorandums on their desks. Unless they were masters at time management or could read quickly, they found themselves overwhelmed.

Today, the same challenge exists, except the memorandums are in electronic form. With the ease of using e-mail, in many respects, the volume of memorandums has become worse.

To lessen the e-mail volume, emphasize that team members use "e-mail etiquette," meaning:

1. Consolidate your messages to the receiver.
2. Ensure that the contents of the message move from major to minor points.
3. Include your name and/or organization on the message.
4. Keep the message to minimum length.
5. Ensure the receiver can print an attached file, if necessary.
6. Use good spelling and grammar.

To reduce the volume of e-mail you receive, you can:

- Distribute a style guide on e-mail and guidelines for everyone on the project.
- Establish a scheme for determining which messages are more important than others (e.g., topic or person).
- Set aside some time during the day to address messages.
- Store messages for later reference onto a hard drive or floppy disk.

In addition, the Web site can be the place to broadcast messages, enable access to databases, and distribute updates to application software.

Despite the advantages of Web technology, it can add to the overall cost of a project. There are several issues the project manager needs to address.

1. Content management. Setting up a Web site is one thing; keeping it current is another. There must be someone on the team to refresh the site to ensure that its content and links stay meaningful.

2. Security. Especially for highly proprietary projects, project managers must restrict access and take measures to prevent a virus from being

downloaded. Firewalls, password protection, and encryption are some ways, but they can be costly.

3. Support. Unless someone already has expertise in Web-related areas (e.g., HTML, Java), then the project manager must train someone or hire the necessary support.

4. Infrastructure. The right technological infrastructure must be in place to use Web technology, including ways to author and deploy documents for the site, hardware with sufficient capacity (e.g., sufficient RAM, processing speed), and software for assessing data created by legacy systems.

5. Productive use. With technological power at their fingertips, team members can be tempted to surf the Internet, which can result in nonproductive time and effort as well as access to unrelated data and software. Project managers must provide standards and guidelines for using this technology, especially on highly visible, politically sensitive projects.

6. Sufficient bandwidth. Web technology goes beyond accessing and transferring text. It involves using static images, audio, video, and data, all of which use bandwidth and challenge the overall capacity of the supporting network infrastructure. Insufficient bandwidth can result in problems like long response time at peak periods of usage.

7. Copyright laws. Placing documents on a Web site may be all right if generated internally, but if the documents have been developed by another organization, issues of fair use and ownership arise.

8. User confidence. Although a key attraction of Web technology is its ease of use, many team members find themselves gun-shy and may experience longer than usual learning curves. Training can help resolve this issue.

The project manager needs to define his requirements upfront, look at the existing technological and knowledge capabilities of his team members, and establish an infrastructure before deciding whether to take advantage of Web technology.

VIDEOCONFERENCING

Videoconferencing once could occur only in a large facility equipped with a vast array of electronic gadgetry. Today, with powerful personal computers and digital networking, videoconferencing takes place on a much smaller scale. Many projects, especially ones with team members spread over a wide geographical area, are increasingly using videoconferencing.

Videoconferencing offers many advantages. It encourages collaboration and communication, and encourages real-time planning rather than relying on passive media like documentation and e-mail. Some major capabilities of PC-based videoconferencing include:

- Multipoint conferencing and point-to-point conferencing
- Providing system diagnostics
- Setting up address books
- Sharing applications
- Transferring files
- Whiteboarding (e.g., electronic diagramming)

However, several challenges remain. The technology is immature, reflected in often blurry, ghostlike, and jerky images. The sound often is not synchronized with the image. Other times, there are incompatibilities between points owing to protocol differences. Sometimes, too, the transmission slows dramatically during high usage periods, causing competition for bandwidth. Finally, preparing for videoconferencing can be costly; the start-up costs alone can be up to three to four times the cost of a workstation.

To get started in videoconferencing, project managers should have a fully configured setup at a sending and receiving site. The technology then includes:

- Additional microcomputers for multiple-site conferences to manage interaction
- Audio board supporting speaking and listening
- Cabling
- Digital camera
- Microcomputer, preferably a Pentium
- Microphone for group interaction; headset for individual interaction
- Modem for phone lines
- Software that provides control settings for audio and video quality; supports standard protocols (e.g., H.320 for ISDN [Integrated Services Digital Network] and H.324 for Plain Old Telephone Service [POTS]); and, sharing applications, transferring data, and whiteboarding
- Videoboard

PROJECT AUTOMATION: RECOGNIZING THE LIMITATIONS

A technological tool like a software package can make managing a project easier and the manager more efficient and effective. However, its use does not guarantee success. Numerous projects have failed although armed with top-notch software. Perry recognizes that a tool does not lead; nor does it define, plan, organize, control, or close a project. People like Perry, and not some silver bullet, do that. Perry realizes, however, that using the right software or other tool—and using it right—helps clear the path to a successful project outcome, and so he selects such tools carefully.

Questions for Getting Started

1. If looking for a project management software package, did you:
   - Define your requirements?
   - Determine how you will go about selecting the package?
   - Consider value-added issues like vendor support? Training? Warranties?
2. If looking for a risk management software package, did you:
   - Define your requirements?
   - Determine how you will go about selecting the package?
   - Determine the type of risk analysis and assessment approach to take?
   - Consider value-added issues like vendor support? Training? Warranties?
3. If you are working in a client/server environment, did you:
   - Determine the necessary hardware and software requirements?
   - Determine the necessary level of technical support?
   - Determine how to deal with issues related to hardware and software performance?
4. If team members are telecommuting, did you:
   - Determine the necessary hardware and software requirements?
   - Determine the necessary level of technical support?
   - Determine how to deal with issues related to hardware and software performance?
5. If team members are using mobile computing, did you:
   - Determine the necessary hardware and software requirements?
   - Determine the necessary level of technical support?
   - Determine how to deal with issues of data backup and recovery? Security? Compatibility of hardware and software as well as distributing upgrades?
6. If team members are using groupware computing, did you:
   - Determine the necessary hardware and software requirements?
   - Determine the necessary level of technical support?
   - Determine ways to overcome hardware and software compatibility and upgrade problems?

7. If team members are using Web technology, did you:
   - Determine the necessary hardware and software requirements?
   - Elect to set up a Web site and determine its layout and contents?
   - Determine what ways to use Web technology (e.g., broadcast messages, access databases)?
   - Determine the necessary level of technical support?
8. If team members are using PC-based videoconferencing, did you:
   - Determine the necessary hardware and software requirements?
   - Determine the necessary level of technical support?
   - Determine the desired uses of the technology (e.g., sharing applications, whiteboarding)?

Appendix:
Case Study
Work Breakdown Structure

1.0 Parties
- 1.1 Bachelor Party
  - 1.1.1 Location
    - 1.1.1.1 Determine location
    - 1.1.1.2 Arrange for facilities
  - 1.1.2 Entertainment/Music
    - 1.1.2.1 Determine type of entertainment/music
    - 1.1.2.2 Arrange for entertainment/music
  - 1.1.3 Food/Beverage
    - 1.1.3.1 Determine type of food/beverage
    - 1.1.3.2 Arrange for food/beverage
  - 1.1.4 Party
    - 1.1.4.1 Conduct bachelor party
- 1.2 Bridal Shower
  - 1.2.1 Location
    - 1.2.1.1 Determine location
    - 1.2.1.2 Arrange for facilities
  - 1.2.2 Entertainment/Music
    - 1.2.2.1 Determine type of entertainment/music
    - 1.2.2.2 Arrange for entertainment/music
  - 1.2.3 Food/Beverage
    - 1.2.3.1 Determine type of food/beverage
    - 1.2.3.2 Arrange for food/beverage
  - 1.2.4 Party
    - 1.2.4.1 Conduct bridal party
- 1.3 Reception
  - 1.3.1 Location
    - 1.3.1.1 Determine location
    - 1.3.1.2 Arrange for facilities

1.3.2   Entertainment/Music
      1.3.2.1   Determine type of entertainment/music
      1.3.2.2   Arrange for entertainment/music
1.3.3   Food/Beverage
      1.3.3.1   Determine type of food/beverage
      1.3.3.2   Arrange for food/beverage
1.3.4   Reception
      1.3.4.1   Conduct reception

2.0   Stationery
  2.1   Invitations
      2.1.1   Bachelor party
         2.1.1.1   Determine whom to invite
         2.1.1.2   Select type of invitation
         2.1.1.3   Mail invitations
      2.1.2   Bridal shower
         2.1.2.1   Determine whom to invite
         2.1.2.2   Select type of invitation
         2.1.2.3   Mail invitations
      2.1.3   Reception
         2.1.3.1   Determine whom to invite
         2.1.3.2   Select type of invitation
         2.1.3.3   Mail invitations
      2.1.4   Wedding
         2.1.4.1   Determine whom to invite
         2.1.4.2   Select type of invitation
         2.1.4.3   Mail invitations
  2.2   Announcement of Engagement
      2.2.1   Select whom to contact (e.g., newspaper)
      2.2.2   Prepare announcement
      2.2.3   Mail announcement to newspapers
  2.3   Thank you cards
      2.3.1   Mail thank you cards for bachelor party
      2.3.2   Mail thank you cards for bridal shower
      2.3.3   Mail thank you cards for reception
      2.3.4   Mail thank you cards for wedding

3.0   Photography/Videography
  3.1   Engagement participants
      3.1.1   Determine portfolio
      3.1.2   Arrange for photographer
      3.1.3   Arrange for videographer
  3.2   Wedding portraits
      3.2.1   Determine portfolio

  3.2.2   Arrange for photographer
  3.2.3   Arrange for videographer
 3.3 Bachelor party
  3.3.1   Arrange for photographer
  3.3.2   Arrange for videographer
 3.4 Bridal shower
  3.4.1   Arrange for photographer
  3.4.2   Arrange for videographer

4.0 Gifts and Favors
 4.1 Bachelor party
  4.1.1   Collect gifts
  4.1.2   Safeguard gifts
  4.1.3   Determine favors
  4.1.4   Distribute favors
 4.2 Bridal shower
  4.2.1   Collect gifts
  4.2.2   Safeguard gifts
  4.2.3   Determine favors
  4.2.4   Distribute favors
 4.3 Reception
  4.3.1   Collect gifts
  4.3.2   Safeguard gifts
  4.3.3   Determine favors
  4.3.4   Distribute favors

5.0 Attire
 5.1 Bride
  5.1.1   Gown
    5.1.1.1   Select gown
    5.1.1.2   Tailor gown
  5.1.2   Headpiece
    5.1.2.1   Select headpiece
    5.1.2.2   Fit headpiece
  5.1.3   Veil
    5.1.3.1   Select veil
    5.1.3.2   Fit veil
  5.1.4   Hairstyle
    5.1.4.1   Select hairstyle
    5.1.4.2   Coordinate with hairstylist
  5.1.5   Makeup
    5.1.5.1   Determine cosmetic requirements
    5.1.5.2   Coordinate with cosmetician

5.2   Groom
    5.2.1   Tuxedo
        5.2.1.1   Select tuxedo
        5.2.1.2   Tailor tuxedo

6.0   Transportation
    6.1   Wedding
        6.1.1   Bride and groom
            6.1.1.1   Identify limousine service to church
            6.1.1.2   Coordinate limousine service to church
            6.1.1.3   Identify limousine service to reception
            6.1.1.4   Coordinate limousine service to reception
        6.1.2   Guests
            6.1.2.1   Determine transportation requirements to church
            6.1.2.2   Coordinate transportation to church
            6.1.2.3   Determine transportation requirements to and from reception
            6.1.2.4   Coordinate transportation requirements to and from reception
            6.1.2.5   Arrange for valet service for church
            6.1.2.6   Arrange for valet service for reception

7.0   Fees
    7.1   Church service
        7.1.1   Pay for church service
    7.2   Parking
        7.2.1   Pay parking fees for wedding
        7.2.2   Pay parking fees for reception

8.0   Flowers
    8.1   Wedding
        8.1.1   Determine floral requirements
        8.1.2   Coordinate floral delivery
        8.1.3   Pay florist
    8.2   Reception
        8.2.1   Determine floral requirements
        8.2.2   Coordinate floral delivery
        8.2.3   Pay florist

9.0   Honeymoon
    9.1   Determine location for honeymoon
    9.2   Arrange for transportation to honeymoon location
    9.3   Arrange lodging for honeymooners

9.4 Develop itinerary for honeymooners
9.5 Depart for honeymoon

10.0 Guests

10.1 Develop guest list
10.2 Coordinate lodging
10.3 Coordinate transportation (ground and air)
10.4 Arrange for food and beverages
10.5 Send letter of contact regarding services

11.0 Flowers

11.1 License
    11.1.1 Prepare wedding license
    11.1.2 Coordinate with civil authorities
11.2 Registry
    11.2.1 Set up registry at church

12.0 Rings

12.1 Engagement ring
    12.1.1 Determine requirements from bride
    12.1.2 Determine requirements from groom
    12.1.3 Coordinate with jeweler
    12.1.4 Deliver ring to bride
12.2 Wedding ring
    12.2.1 Determine requirements from bride
    12.2.2 Determine requirements from groom
    12.2.3 Coordinate with jeweler
    12.2.4 Deliver ring to bride
    12.2.5 Deliver ring to groom

13.0 Lighting

13.1 Wedding
    13.1.1 Determine lighting requirements at church
    13.1.2 Coordinate lighting requirements at church
    13.1.3 Install lighting at church
13.2 Reception
    13.2.1 Determine lighting requirements
    13.2.2 Coordinate lighting requirements
    13.2.3 Install lighting

14.0 Rules

14.1 Wedding
    14.1.1 Identify bridesmaids
    14.1.2 Identify best man

14.1.3 Identify maid of honor

14.1.4 Identify flower girls

14.1.5 Identify ring bearers

14.1.6 Identify ushers

14.2 Reception

14.2.1 Identify who will be in receiving line

14.2.2 Identify who will toast the newlyweds

15.0 Decorations

15.1 Wedding

15.1.1 Determine decoration requirements for church

15.1.2 Coordinate set up of decorations at church

15.1.3 Set up decorations at church

15.2 Reception

15.2.1 Determine decoration requirements at reception area

15.2.2 Coordinate set up of decorations at reception area

15.2.3 Set up decorations at reception area

16.0 Food/Beverages

16.1 Reception

16.1.1 Determine food requirements

16.1.2 Coordinate food delivery

16.1.3 Coordinate serving of food

16.1.4 Determine alcoholic and nonalcoholic beverages

16.1.5 Coordinate beverage delivery

16.1.6 Coordinate serving of beverages

17.0 Church

17.1 Contact church of choice regarding date, time, and number of attendees

17.2 Coordinate with church specific requirements regarding service

17.3 Conduct wedding

18.0 Cake

18.1 Determine requirements for cake

18.2 Submit requirements to bakery

18.3 Arrange for delivery of cake to reception area

18.4 Coordinate serving of cake

19.0 Rehearsals

19.1 Wedding

19.1.1 Coordinate with church the date and time of rehearsals

19.1.2 Coordinate with wedding party the date and time of rehearsals

19.1.3 Conduct first wedding rehearsal

19.1.4 Conduct second wedding rehearsal

19.2 Reception

19.2.1 Coordinate with reception area owner the date and time of rehearsals

19.2.2 Coordinate with receiving line and toaster the date and time of rehearsals

19.2.3 Conduct first reception rehearsal

19.2.4 Conduct second reception rehearsal

Glossary of Project Management Terms

active listening   Genuinely hearing what the speaker says.

actual cost of work performed (ACWP)   The actual costs accrued for one or more tasks up to a specific point in time.

arrow diagram   A charting approach that uses nodes to represent events and arrows to describe the task between the nodes.

assessing status   Determining how well the project has and will achieve its goals and objectives.

backward pass   Using the durations and dependencies in a network diagram, and moving from right to left through a network diagram, beginning with the very last task, to calculate the late start and finish dates.

bar or Gantt chart   A charting approach that displays a list of tasks and, for each one, an accompanying bar to reflect the flow time or duration.

baseline   Agreed-upon points of reference. In a project environment, baselines are set for schedule, budget, and quality.

body language   The physical movements that account for 70 to 90 percent of our conversation (e.g., facial expressions, body movements, posture, and eye movements).

budgeted cost for work performed (BCWP)   The estimated value of the work completed up to a specific point in time.

budgeted cost for work scheduled (BCWS)   The estimated value of the work scheduled.

burdened labor rates   Rates that include the cost of fringe benefits (e.g., insurance, floor space, nonlabor overhead).

cause and effect diagram   A charting approach to identify the cause of a problem by identifying the interrelationships among the four M's: *m*achines, *m*anpower, *m*aterials, and *m*ethods.

change, corrective   Revisions that are nice to have but unnecessary.

change, high-priority   Revisions that demand immediate attention.

change, low-priority   Revisions that are addressed, if time permits.

change, major   Revisions that dramatically affect schedule, cost, or quality.

change, medium-priority   Revisions that do not require immediate attention.

change, minor   Revisions that do not fit in the major change category.

change board   The people responsible for classifying and prioritizing changes.

checkpoint review   A type of session held at specific times, usually after a red-letter date or significant event (e.g., completion of a major milestone).

checksheet   Document that records the frequency distribution of a number of incidents.

client/server environment   A computing architecture where some or all application processing may reside at the client (e.g., microcomputer level) or be shared with a server (e.g., mini- or mainframe computer level).

closing   A function of project management that involves compiling statistics, releasing people, and preparing lessons learned.

component   A basic element of a system.

concept phase   The first phase of the project cycle. During this phase, the idea of a project arises and preliminary cost and schedule estimates are developed at a high level to determine if the project is technically and economically feasible.

constraint date   The time mandating that a task may have to begin or finish on or by a specific date.

contingency planning   Tentative responses to situations that have a good probability of occurrence and could impact project performance.

control (n.)   A measure in place to mitigate, prevent, or correct the impact of a threat.

control chart   A diagram that identifies normal and anomalous situations—specifically a variance from an average.

controlling   The function of project management that assesses how well a project meets its goals and objectives. It involves collecting and assessing status, managing changes to baselines, and responding to circumstances that can negatively impact project performance.

corrective action   Steps taken to get the project back on track.

cost variance   The difference between budgeted and actual costs.

critical path   One or more paths through the network diagram with tasks having zero float.

data flow   A diagramming technique showing the flow of data through a system.

defining   The function of project management that determines exactly the purpose and boundaries of a project. It involves determining the overall vision, goals, objectives, scope, responsibilities, and deliverables of a project.

delegating   Having a person act on behalf of another individual.

direct costs   Charges directly related to the building of a product (e.g., materials and specialized labor).

dissatisfier   Psychological desire that if not satisfied will negatively impact motivation.

distributed computing   A computing environment where processing power is split among different levels in systems architecture.

diversity   A work environment tolerating a variety of backgrounds, including race, nationality, ethnicity, and religion.

duration   The flow time of a task.

early finish date   The earliest time a task can be completed.

earned value   The integration of cost and schedule to determine the level of progress.

effectiveness   Whether a project is achieving its goals and objectives.

efficiency   Whether a project is consuming more or fewer resources than expected.

expectancy theory   Successful performance depends on the expectations of rewards, whether extrinsic or intrinsic, that a person has.

expected time   Using the most likely, most optimistic, and most pessimistic variables to calculate the time anticipated to complete a task.

feedback loop   The flow of information between the project manager, team members, the customer, and senior management.

finish-to-finish dependency   The relationship between tasks whereby they must finish around the same time.

finish-to-start dependency   The relationship between tasks whereby an earlier activity, or predecessor, completes before the next one, or successor, can begin.

fixed cost   Unalterable charge owing to changes in work volume (e.g., cost of facilities usage).

float, free   The time that an activity can slide without impacting the start date of its successor. Tasks with free float appear on the noncritical path.

float, total   The time that an activity can slide without impacting the project completion date.

flowchart   Pictures and diagrams used for displaying processes and procedures.

form   Document that captures and communicates information; useful for providing audit trails.

formulation phase   A time in a project cycle when complete project plans are developed, which include a statement of work, work breakdown structure, and schedule.

forward pass   Using durations and dependencies in a network diagram and moving from left to right through a network diagram, beginning with the very first task to calculate the early start and finish dates.

Gantt chart   *See* bar chart.

global efficiency factor (GEF) estimate   A technique that incorporates nonproductive time into an estimate.

groupware computing   A computing environment allowing the sharing of applications and data.

hierarchy of needs   A psychological model of motivation developed by Abraham Maslow. It identifies people's needs according to this hierarchical order: physiological (food), safety (shelter), social (acceptance), esteem (sense of importance), and self-actualization (becoming).

histogram   A graphical depiction of resources being or that have been utilized. The high points are called peaks and low points are called valleys.

histogram, leveled   A histogram with the extreme peaks and valleys smoothed out.

histogram, unleveled   A histogram with an irregular shape, consisting of many peaks and valleys.

implementation phase   A time in a project cycle when the execution of the plan achieves the goals and objectives.

indirect cost   Charge not necessarily related to the building of a product (e.g., rent and taxes).

installation phase   A time in a project cycle when the final product is delivered to the customer.

Internet technology   Electronic technology that ties together communities throughout an organization.

intranet Basically the same computing technology as that used to operate the Internet. The primary difference between the two is that an intranet uses a firewall, or server, to regulate or screen communications.

item-by-item format procedure Procedural documentation that contains a mixture of topics.

job enlargement Increasing the number of tasks and responsibilities to perform on a job.

job enrichment Structuring or assigning tasks and responsibilities to give a person the opportunity to actualize.

job rotation Moving a person from one job to another to increase his overall awareness or exposure.

key project indicator (KPI) Element of a project that contributes to its successful completion.

lag The gap between the end of one task and the start of another.

late finish date The latest time a task can be completed.

late start date The latest time a task can begin.

leading The only function of project management that simultaneously occurs when executing the other five functions. It involves inspiring people to accomplish goals and objectives at a level that meets or exceeds expectations.

lessons learned document A medium for capturing the successes, challenges, and other information of a project.

maintenance factor A dissatisfier, meaning that if not present to a sufficient degree, it will negatively impact motivation.

management estimate at completion (MEAC) A combination of actual expenditures to date plus the remaining estimate to complete the project.

management reserve A fund set aside to address unexpected costs, usually 3 to 5 percent of the total estimate for the project.

managerial level The detail that is "rolled up" to higher levels for reporting purposes, usually the higher levels in the work breakdown structure.

matrix structure Resources from functional organizations that are shared with other projects.

mean The average of the values for items in a group of data.

median A position average at the midpoint for a frequency distribution.

meeting, ad hoc   A type of meeting that is held irregularly, often spontaneously, by team members.

meeting, staff   A type of session that is held regularly. All team members
meet to receive information from the project manager and to share
additional data and insights.

memo   A brief document that should contain a date, subject title, addressee, signature block, purpose statement; it should also answer the
who, what, when, where, and why of a subject.

metrics   Tools and techniques to determine standards and track against
them.

metrics, qualitative   Intangible, noncalibrated measures that are subjective.

metrics, quantitative   Tangible, calibrated measures that are objective.

Michigan studies   Management research that revealed two types of supervisory styles that can affect motivation: production and employee
centered.

milestone chart   The outlay on a Gantt chart that shows an icon or symbol for the occurrence of an event rather than a bar for durations.

mobile computing   An information systems environment that enables
team members to work at remote locations and provide timely results.

mode   The value that appears most frequently in a series of numbers.

monitoring   Projecting into the future using past performance.

most likely estimate   The effort (usually in hours) to complete a task
under normal or reasonable conditions.

most optimistic estimate   The effort to complete a task under the best
or ideal circumstances.

most pessimistic estimate   The effort to complete a task under the
worst conceivable circumstances.

motivational factor   A satisfier, meaning psychological desire that if addressed will positively impact performance.

Myers-Briggs type indicator   A psychological tool that identifies personality types based on the combination of four preferences: extrovert
versus introvert; sensing versus intuitive; thinking versus feeling; and
judging versus perceiving.

n Ach   A theory by David C. McClelland that found people have a need to
achieve; the degree varies from person to person.

narrative format procedure   Procedural documentation that communicates information in essay style.

network diagram A chart displaying the logical relationships, or dependencies, between the tasks.

newsletter A communications tool that keeps everyone abreast of important happenings and information. It serves as a record of activities and accomplishments.

ninety (90) percent syndrome 90 percent of a project is completed, while the last 10 percent consumes most of the flow time.

nonburdened rate The labor cost minus the cost of fringe benefits and overhead.

nonrecurring costs A charge that appears only once (e.g., the purchase of equipment).

organizing A function of project management that orchestrates the use of resources cost-effectively to execute plans. It involves activities like assembling a team, clarifying relationships among parties, preparing procedures, creating a project manual, and setting up project history files.

overrun A positive value for total estimate-at-completion.

overtime labor rate The charge that exceeds 40 hours per week, including time and a half and double time.

Pareto chart A diagram that displays information to determine the potential causes of a problem.

participative management A managerial approach for getting people involved by getting their input or feedback prior to making a decision.

personality The composite set of characteristics that make up a person's behavior.

planning A function of project management that determines the steps needed to execute a project, assigns who will perform them, and identifies their start and completion dates.

playscript format procedure Procedural documentation that is similar to the sequential format. It is best used for procedures involving two or more people.

precedence diagramming method *See* program evaluation and review technique.

predecessor task A task that precedes the occurrence of another task.

procedures Documentation that provides detailed information on performing tasks.

product breakdown structure (PBS) A delineation of the segments that constitute the final product or service.

productivity adjustment percent (PAP) An estimating approach that applies the global efficiency factor on a larger scale. It involes applying an overall productivity factor to the estimate for all tasks.

program evaluation and review technique (PERT) A precedence diagramming method often used in nonconstruction environments (e.g., information systems, pharmaceutical, and engineering industries). It uses three estimates to complete a task: most likely, most pessimistic, and most optimistic.

project A discrete set of tasks performed in a logical sequence to attain a specific result. Each task and the entire project have a start and stop date.

project announcement A memo that is widely distributed to announce the beginning of a project.

project communications Establishing an infrastructure for disseminating information. It involves setting up the project office, establishing and conducting appropriate meetings, giving effective presentations, and applying interpersonal skills.

project cycle The set of phases for completing a project.

project history file A drawer in a filing cabinet, a directory on a personal computer, or file server that stores important documentation.

project leadership Inspiring people to perform in a manner that meets or exceeds expectations.

project library A central means for storing information.

project management The tools, knowledge, and techniques used to lead, define, plan, organize, control, and close a project.

project management, classical approach The use of three standard items (cost, schedule, and quality) to determine the success of a project.

project manager the person who interacts with myriad people (e.g., sponsors, senior management, client, and team members) to achieve the goals of a project.

project manual A compendium of reference material for a project.

project office A central location established to manage a project.

quality A service or product that satisfies the requirements and expectations of the customer.

reading people Understanding the true motives of people by their actions.

recurring cost Charge that appears regularly (e.g., long-term payments for facilities).

regular labor rates   The wage rate amount earned for less than or equal to 40 hours per week.

replanning   Redoing the project plan by making wholesale changes to cost, schedule, and quality.

report   A feedback mechanism to communicate information.

resource allocation   The distribution of materials, labor, etc., among tasks.

resource profile   A graphic display of the planned or actual use of one or more resources over the duration of one or more tasks.

risk, acceptable   Allowing a threat to negatively affect a task on the non-critical path.

risk, external   A threat that originates from outside the scope of a project.

risk, internal   A threat that originates from inside the scope of a project.

risk, long-term   A threat that has an impact in the distant future.

risk, manageable   A threat that can be managed.

risk, short-term   A threat that has an immediate impact.

risk, unacceptable   A threat that negatively affects a task on the critical path.

risk, unmanageable   A threat that can't be managed.

risk acceptance   Accepting a risk rather than preventing or mitigating its impact.

risk adaptation   Taking measures that will mitigate a risk's impact.

risk analysis   Identifying the components of a project, its risks, and the controls that should be or are in place.

risk avoidance   Taking action that will keep a risk from seriously impacting a project.

risk control   Deciding what action to take to prevent or mitigate the impact of a risk.

risk evaluation   Collecting information and determining the adequacy of controls.

risk identification   Recognizing the major elements of a project and their associated risks.

risk management   The process of identifying, analyzing, controlling, and reporting risk.

risk management, qualitative   An approach for managing risks that relies on judgments using criteria to determine outcomes.

risk management, quantitative   An approach for managing risks that relies mainly on statistical calculation to determine risks and their probability of occurrence.

risk reporting   Informing team members and senior management of risks and their associated controls.

risk transfer   Letting someone else assume a risk.

rules of exchange   Communications etiquette.

satisfier   Psychological desire that, if addressed, will have a positive impact on performance.

scattergram   A graphic that shows the relationship between two variables. Sometimes called a scatter or correlation chart.

schedule variance   The difference between planned and actual start and end dates.

scheduling   Logically sequencing tasks and then calculating start and stop dates for each one. The result of scheduling is a diagram showing the logical sequence and the calculated dates.

scientific management   Identifying the most efficient tasks to perform a job, train people on them, develop standards to measure performance, and separate work between management and workers.

scientific wildly assumed guess (SWAG) estimate   The most popular but most unreliable estimating technique. It requires making one-time estimates to complete a task.

sequential format procedure   Procedural document that presents information.

social style matrix   A psychological or sociological tool that divides social styles and personal expectations based upon two dimensions, assertiveness and responsiveness.

span of control   The number of people that a project manager can effectively manage.

standard deviation   The degree that each occurrence in a frequency distribution is located from the mean. It measures dispersion.

start-to-start dependency   The relationship between tasks whereby two or more of them begin around the same time.

statement of understanding (SOU)   An informal statement of work.

statement of work (SOW)   An agreement between the customer and project's leadership on the exact definition of the project.

status review   A type of session to collect information to determine progress against cost, schedule, and quality criteria set for a project.

steering committee   A group of people providing general oversight of and guidance of the project.

stretching   Assigning people to tasks that challenge them.

successor task   An activity that starts after the completion of a previous one.

sustaining phase   A time in a project life cycle where the product is under the customer's cognizance and an infrastructure exists to maintain and enhance it.

synergy   The output of a group, usually greater than the sum of the individual inputs.

task breakdown structure (TBS)   A top-down listing of tasks to build a part or perform an aspect of a service.

task force structure   A group of people assembled who are dedicated to completing a specific goal.

technical level   The lower level of the work breakdown structure that contains the actual tasks to perform, which will be used for rollups when reporting to management.

telecommuting   People participating on projects using personal computers at their homes.

Theory X   A style of management that takes a negative view of human nature.

Theory Y   A style of management that takes a positive view of human nature.

threat   The occurrence of an event that negatively affects a project.

tracking   Looking at past performance.

trend chart   A graphical chart to display past performance and forecast results based upon the history.

underrun   A negative value for total estimate-at-completion.

variable cost   The charge that varies depending upon consumption and workload.

variance   The difference between what is planned and what has actually occurred up to a specific point in time.

videoconferencing   People interacting across geographical regions using video as the medium.

visibility wall or room   A place where all project documentation and other related information are showcased.

vision   An idea of a desired result in the future.

vision statement   A document describing what the project will achieve.

vulnerability   The inherent degree of weakness of components.

work breakdown structure (WBS)   A detailed listing of the deliverables and tasks for building a product or delivering a service. It is top-down, broad-to-specific, and hierarchical.

work package level   The tasks or subtasks that will be used for assigning responsibilities, constructing schedules, and tracking progress. It is the lowest level in the work breakdown structure.

References

Books

Bennaton, E. M. *On Time, Within Budget.* New York: Wiley-QED, 1992.

Bennis, Warren, and Burt Nanus. *Leaders.* New York: Harper and Row, 1985.

Blake, Robert R., and Anne Adams McCanse. *Leadership Dilemmas—Grid Solutions.* Houston, Tex.: Gulf Publishing, 1991.

Block, Robert. *The Politics of Projects.* New York: Yourdon Press, 1983.

Bramson, Robert. *Coping with Difficult People.* New York: Dell, 1981.

Briner, Wendy, Michael Geddes, and Colin Hastings. *Project Leadership.* Brookfield, Vt.: Gower, 1990.

Champy, James. *Reengineering Management.* New York: Harper Business, 1995.

DeMarco, Tom. *Controlling Software Projects.* Englewood Cliffs, N.J.: Yourdon press, 1982.

DeMarco, Tom, and Timothy Lister. *Peopleware.* New York: Dorset House Publishing, 1987.

Deming, W. Edwards. *Out of the Crisis.* Cambridge, Mass.: MIT Press, 1986.

Donnelly, James H. Jr., James L. Gibson, and John M. Ivancevich. *Fundamentals of Management.* Plano, Tex.: Business Publications, 1981.

Drucker, Peter F. *Management.* New York: Harper Colophon Books, 1985.

———. *The Practice of Management.* New York: Harper and Row, 1982.

Duyn, J. Van. *The DP Professional's Guide to Writing Effective Technical Communications.* New York: Wiley-Interscience, 1982.

FitzGerald, Jerry, and Arda F. Fitzgerald. *Designing Controls into Competitive Systems,* 2nd ed. Jerry FitzGerald and Associates: Redwood City, Calif., 1990.

Gannon, Martin J. Management: *An Organizational Perspective.* Boston: Little, Brown, 1977.

GAO. *Assessing Risks and Returns: A Guide for Evaluating Federal Agencies' IT Investment Decision-making.* GAO/AIMD-10.1.13, February 1997.

――――. *Tax Systems Modernization, Statement of Gene L. Dodaro.* GAO/T-AIMD-96-75, March 26, 1996.

――――. *Tax Systems Modernization.* GAO/AIMD-95-156, July 1995.

Garfield, Charles. *Peak Performers.* New York: Morrow, 1986.

Guidelines for Automatic Data Process Risk Analysis. FIPS Pub 65, August 1, 1979.

Harper, Ann, and Bob Harper. *Skill-Building for Self-Directed Team Members.* New York: MW Corporation, 1994.

Imai, Masaaki. *Kaizen: The Key to Japan's Competitive Success.* New York: McGraw-Hill, 1986.

James, Muriel, and Dorothy Jongeward. *Born to Win.* Reading, Mass.: Addison-Wesley, 1987.

Juran, J. M. *Juran on Leadership for Quality.* New York: The Free Press, 1989.

――――. *Juran on Quality by Design.* New York: The Free Press, 1992.

Keirsey, David, and Marilyn Bates. *Please Understand Me.* Del Mar, Calif.: Prometheus Nemesis Book Company, 1984.

Kerzner, Harold. *Project Management,* 5th ed. New York: Van Nostrand Reinhold, 1995.

Kliem, Ralph L. *AHI's Productivity Sourcebook.* New York: Alexander Hamilton Institute, 1988.

Kliem, Ralph L., and Irwin S. Ludin. *DP Manager's Model Reports and Formats.* Englewood Cliffs, N.J.: Prentice Hall, 1992.

――――. *Just-In-Time Systems for Computing Environments.* Westport, Conn.: Quorum Books, 1994.

――――. *The Noah Project.* Brookfield, Vt.: Gower, 1993.

――――. *The People Side of Project Management.* Brookfield, Vt.: Gower, 1994.

――――. *Stand and Deliver.* Brookfield, Vt.: Gower, 1995.

Kouzes, James M., and Barry Z. Posner. *The Leadership Challenge.* San Francisco: Jossey-Bass, 1988.

McFarland, Dalton E. *Management: Principles and Practices,* 4th ed. New York: Macmillan, 1974.

Nirenberg, Jesse S. *Getting Through to People.* Englewood Cliffs, N.J.: Prentice Hall, 1979.

Orsburn, Jack D., Linda Moran, Ed Musselwhite, and John H. Zenger. *Self-Directed Work Teams.* Homewood, Ill.: Business One Irwin, 1990.

Productivity Management, 2nd ed. Boston: Keane, 1995.

Project Management Institute Standards Committee. *A Guide to the Project Management Body of Knowledge.* Upper Darby, Pa.: 1996.

Salton, Gary J. *Organizational Engineering.* Ann Arbor, Mich.: Professional Communications, 1996.

Scheduling Guide for Program Managers. Fort Belvoir, Va.: Defense Systems Management College, October 1986.

Schonberger, Richard J. *Japanese Manufacturing Techniques.* New York: The Free Press, 1982.

Stewart, Dorothy M. *Handbook of Management Skills.* Brookfield, Vt.: Gower, 1987.

Synnott, William R., and William H. Gruber. *Information Resource Management.* New York: Wiley-Interscience, 1981.

Ulrich, David, and Dale Lake. *Organizational Capability.* New York: Wiley, 1990.

MAGAZINES

Adhikari, Richard. "Developers Benefit from a Process Blueprint." *Software Magazine,* March 1996.

Angus, Jeff. "State Scraps IS Project." *Information Week,* March 24, 1997.

———. "Projects Get Kick Start." *Computerworld,* December 4, 1995.

Anthes, Gary. "White House Ultimatum to Fed IS: Shape Up Systems or Lose Funding." *Computerworld,* November 18, 1996.

Bach, James. "Enough About Process: What We Need Are Heroes." *IEEE Software,* March 1995.

Barbour, Doug. "What Makes a Good Project Fail." *Object Magazine,* September 1996.

Bartholomew, Doug. "California Chaos." *Information Week,* May 6, 1996.

———. "Visual Schedules." *Information Week,* May 27, 1996.

Baum, David. "New Technology Burnout?" *Datamation,* November 15, 1995.

Bemowski, Karen. "Leaders on Leadership." *Quality Progress,* January 1996.

———. "What Makes American Teams Tick?" *Quality Progress,* January 1995.

Bennis, Warren. "Managing People Is Like Herding Cats." *Executive Book Summaries,* March 1997.

————. "Why Leaders Can't Lead." *Training and Development Journal*, April 1989.

Betts, Mitch. "IS Model Addresses 'Peopleware' Issues." *Computerworld*, January 23, 1995.

Booker, Ellis. "No Silver Bullet for IS Projects." *Computerworld*, July 11, 1994.

Bredin, Alice. "Coping Without Boundaries." *Computerworld*, November 15, 1993.

Breen, Tim. "Cultural Project Management." *PM Network*, September 1996.

Bridges, Linda. "Wanted: Personable MIS and IS People." *PC Week*, September 12, 1996.

Brown, Connie S. "Traveling the Road of Management." *Network World*, July 7, 1997.

Brownstein, Barry. "Using Project Templates to Improve New Product Development." *PM Network*, March 1996.

Bukowitz, Wendi. "In The Know." *CIO*, April 15, 1996.

Bullea, Christine V. "Reexamining Productivity CSFs." *Information Systems Management*, Summer 1995.

Butler, Janet. "Automating Process Trims Software Development Fat." *Software Magazine*, August 1994.

Cabanis, Jeannette. "1996 Project Management Software Survey." *PM Network*, September 1996.

Cafasso, Rosemary. "Few IS Projects Come In On Time, On Budget." *Computerworld*, December 12, 1994.

————. "Satisfaction Guaranteed." *Computerworld*, November 20, 1995.

————. "Selling Your Soft Side." *Computerworld*, April 1, 1996.

Caldwell, Bruce. "Taming the Beast." *Information Week*, March 10, 1997.

————. "Top Execs Take IT Reins." *Information Week*, March 17, 1997.

Calonius, Erik. "Take Me to Your Leader." *Hemispheres*, April 1995.

Camerato, Carlos R. "A Brazilian Project Management Case." *PM Network*, September 1996.

Caminiti, Susan. "What Team Leaders Need to Know." *Fortune*, February 20, 1995.

Campbell, Richard. "Create Reports That Get Rave Reviews." *Data Based Advisor*, April 1996.

Capozzoli, Dr. Thomas K. "Resolving Conflict Within Teams." *Journal for Quality and Participation*, December 1995.

Carey, Jean. "Successful Strategies for Estimating Projects." *Tech Exec,* March 1990.

Caudron, Shari. "Strategies for Managing Creative Workers." *Personnel Journal,* December 1994.

Collins, Mary Ellen. "High-Performance Teams and Their Impact on Organizations." *Journal for Quality and Participation,* December 1995.

Companis, Nicholas A. "Delphi: Not the Greek Oracle, but Close." *PM Network,* February 1997.

Cone, Edward. "The Mess at IRS." *Information Week,* April 15, 1996.

Constantine, Larry L. "Consensus and Compromise." *Computer Language,* April 1992.

―――. "Dealing With Difficult People." *Software Development,* June 1997.

Corlini, James. "A Trustworthy Cynic." *Network World,* October 14, 1996.

Covey, Stephen R. "The Quadrant of Quality." *Quality Digest,* July 1995.

Crom, Steven, and Herbert France. "Teamwork Brings Breakthrough Improvements in Quality and Climate." *Quality Progress,* March 1996.

Crowley, Aileen. "The New Metrics." *PC Week,* November 28, 1994.

Csenger, Michael. "Staying the Course." *Network World,* July 7, 1997.

Currey, Jane. "Project Sponsorship." *PMI Network,* March 1995.

Dancause, Richard. "The Best of Both Worlds: Project Management with Consultants and In-House Staff." *PM Network,* March 1997.

DeBono, Edward. "Serious Creativity." *Journal for Quality and Participation,* September 1995.

Delavigne, Kenneth T. "How to Distinguish the Masters from the Hacks." *Quality Progress,* May 1995.

Dellecave, Tom, Jr. "It's About Time." *Information Week,* May 1, 1995.

Dern, Daniel. "Tech Savvy Alone Won't Get You to the Top." *Network World,* May 26, 1997.

Dettmer, H. William. "Quality and the Theory of Constraints." *Quality Progress,* April 1995.

DeVoe, Deborah. "Project Updates Tracks Status." *InfoWorld,* October 10, 1995.

Dew, John. "Creating Team Leaders." *Journal for Quality and Participation,* October/November 1995.

Dimancescu, Dan, and Kemp Dwenger. "Smoothing the Product Development Path." *Management Review,* January 1996.

Dinsmore, Paul C. "Tom Peters Is Behind the Times." *PM Network,* September 1996.

————. "Lining Up the Corporate Ducks." *PM Network,* February 1997.

Due, Richard T. "The Knowledge Economy." *Information Systems Management,* Summer 1995.

Durrenberger, Mark. "Using Modern Project Management Tools to Build a Project Team." *PM Network,* March 1996.

Durrenberger, Mark, Beebe Nelson, and Steve Spring. "Managing the External Forces in New Product Development." *PM Network,* March 1996.

Edgemom, Jim. "Right Stuff: How to Recognize It When Selecting a Project Manager." *Application Development Trends,* May 1995.

Engler, Natalie. "Are Your Projects Under Control." *Open Computing,* August 1985.

————. "Break Out the Champagne, It's a Crisis." *Computerworld,* July 15, 1996.

————. "Coming Together." *Computerworld,* November 25, 1996.

————. "Stressed." *Computerworld,* April 15, 1996.

Fabris, Peter. "Ground Control." *CIO,* April 1, 1996.

————. "The Water Cooler." *CIO,* October 15, 1996.

Fairley, Richard. "Risk Management for Software Projects." *Data Processing Digest,* August 1994.

Fallen, Howard. "The Implementation Coordinator: The Project Manager's Ally." *PM Network,* May 1995.

Farkas, Charles M., and Suzy Wetlaufer. "The Ways Chief Executives Lead." *Review,* May-June 1996.

Faulkner Technical Reports. "ABT Project Workbench" *(MIC2.3840.020),* February 1995.

————. "Primavera Project Planner." *(MIC2.3840.100),* February 1995.

————. "Project Management Software: Product Summaries." *(509.0000.210),* 1995.

Filipczak, Bob. "It Takes All Kinds: Creativity in the Work Force." *Training,* May 1997.

Finekirsh, Sidney. "Management by Measurement." *Enterprise Systems Journal,* January 1995.

Fleming, Quentin W., Joel M. Koppelman. "Taking Step Four With Earned Value: Establish the Project Baseline." *PM Network,* May 1995.

Fryer, Bronwyn. "Separation Anxiety." *Computerworld,* November 14, 1994.

Garner, Rochelle. "Family Feud." *Computerworld,* November 21, 1994.

Gibbs, Mark. "Foraging in the Team Toolbox." *Network World,* January/February 1996.

Gilb, Tom. "Software Metrics and the Result Method." *American Programmer,* December 1995.

Githens, Gregory D. "Creating Value in Product Innovation." *PM Network,* March 1996.

Goff, Leslie. "The Rise of the Generalist Guru." *Client/Server Journal,* June 1996.

Greenberg, Ilan. "CA-Superproject Uses ODBC, Manages Multiple Projects." *InfoWorld,* October 10, 1995.

Greene, Tim. "Telecommuting Is More Than Hardware and Software." *Network World,* July 7, 1997.

Griffin, Jane. "Building Bridges, Not Rivalries." *PM Network,* August 1996.

Hamilton, Neil. "Reducing Project Risk: Defining Requirements." *Enterprise Systems Journal,* September 1995.

————. "Reducing Project Risk: Planning the Project." *Enterprise Systems Journal,* March 1995.

Harari, Oren. "The Dream Team." *Management Review,* October 1995.

————. "Mind Matters." *Management Review,* January 1996.

Hare, Lynne B., Roger W. Hoerl, John Hromi, and Ronald D. Snee. "The Role of Statistical Thinking in Management." *Quality Progress,* February 1995.

Harmon, James F. "The Supervisor and Quality Control Circles." *Supervisory Management,* March 1984.

Harrell, Clayton. "Heuristic Planning Makes the Past Current." *Electronic Design,* April 15, 1996.

Harris, Richard M. "Turn Listening Into a Powerful Presence." *Training Development,* July 1997.

Hart, Julie. "Pesky Projects." *Computerworld,* April 11, 1994.

————. "Successful Systems Analysts: User Friendly." *Computerworld,* February 26, 1996.

Hauss, Deborah. "Writing and Communications Remain Top Priorities." *Public Relations Journal,* October 1995.

Hayes, Frank. "IS Users Take Team Approach." *Computerworld,* October 23, 1995.

Hayes, Steve. "Strategies for First-Project Success." *Object Magazine,* December 1996.

Heck, Mike. "TurboProject's a Bargain for Midrange Planners." *InfoWorld,* September 23, 1996.

Heifetz, Ronald A., and Donald L. Laurie. "The Work of Leadership," *Harvard Business Review,* January-February 1997.

Henry, Bill. "Measuring IS for Business Value." *Datamation,* April 1, 1990.

Hildebrand, Carol. "All Together Now." *CIO,* March 1, 1996.

———. "I'm Okay, You're Really Weird." *CIO,* October 1, 1995.

———. "A Road Map for Risk." *CIO,* April 15, 1996.

Hill, Cheryl. "7 Tips for Effective International Writing." *Competitive Edge,* Winter 1996.

Holland, Neila A. "Participative Management." *Journal for Quality and Participation,* September 1995.

Holpp, Lawrence. "Teams: It's All That Planning." *Training and Development,* April 1997.

Horowitz, Alan S. "Hey, Listen Up!" *Computerworld,* July 1, 1996.

———. "The Leader." *Computerworld,* October 28, 1996.

Inderman, Kurt. "Behind the Lines." *Internet Systems,* July 1997.

Jaycox, Michael. "How to Get Nonbelievers to Participate in Teams." *Quality Progress,* March 1996.

Jensen, Christian A. "Project Manager's On-Ramp to the Information Superhighway." *PM Network,* October 1996.

Johnson, Jim. "Chaos: The Dollar Drain of IT Project Failures." *Application Development Trends,* January 1995.

Joint Logistics Commanders Joint Group on Systems Engineering. "The Best Measurement Practices." *Managing Systems Development,* July 1996.

Jones, Capers. "Determining Software Schedules." *Computer,* February 1995.

———. "Hardware Problems of Software Measurement." *Application Development Tools,* May 1995.

Kay, Emily. "Learning the True Value of Creativity." *LAN Times,* September 30, 1996.

Keane, John F. "A Holistic View of Project Management." *AS/400 Systems Management,* June 1996.

Kelly, David. "Project Management Morals." *Client/Server Journal,* date unknown.

Kern, Jill P. "The Chicken Is Involved, But the Pig Is Committed." *Quality Progress,* October 1995.

Keuffel, Warren. "Estimating Projects: Benefits of Dynamic Calibration." *Software Development,* May 1997.

Khan, Saad. "Project Management Package Puts Highway Plan in Fast Lane." *PC Week,* October 17, 1994.

King, Julia. "How to Build a Team with Basic Instinct." *Computerworld,* August 12, 1996.

―――. "IS Reins in Runaway Projects." *Computerworld,* February 24, 1997.

King, Nelson H. "On Time and On Budget." *PC Magazine,* April 11, 1995.

Kliem, Ralph L. "Does Overtime Lead to Greater Productivity?" *Machine Design,* April 7, 1988.

―――. "Giving Presentations That Count." *Leadership for the Front Lines,* February 10, 1997 (No. 299).

―――. "Keeping Warehousing Projects on Track." *Auerbach,* 1996 (21-10-13).

―――. "Making Presentations That Command Attention." *Machine Design,* April 9, 1987.

―――. "Memo-Writing Made Easy." *Machine Design,* August 20, 1987.

―――. "Off to a Good Start." *Data Training,* November 1988.

―――. "Office Memos: Writing Them Right." *Supervisor's Bulletin,* September 30, 1991.

―――. "Overview of Outsourcing." *Faulkner Technical Reports,* March 1992 (100.0000404).

―――. "People: The Missing Ingredient of Effective Management." *PM Network,* January 1989.

―――. "Project Proficiency." *Computerworld,* July 22, 1991.

―――. "Project Success: More Than Just Technical Skill." *High-Tech Manager's Bulletin,* August 25, 1988.

―――. "Recognition Sparks Engineer Motivation." *Machine Design,* February 11, 1988.

―――. "Take Me Out to the Project . . ." *PM Network,* April 1997.

―――. "Ten Keys to Productive Meetings." *Data Communications,* November 1986.

―――. "Ten Steps to More Effective Speaking." *Supervisor's Bulletin,* August 15, 1988.

―――. "Ten Ways to Insure a Software Project." *Tech Exec,* September 1989.

―――. "The Missing Ingredient." *Machine Design,* March 23, 1989.

―――. "Total Quality Management." *Faulkner Information Services,* July 1994 (os2.4410.025).

―――. "Using Project Management to Put Client/Server Projects Back on Track." *Information Strategy,* Winter 1997.

―――. "Using Project Management to Put Reengineering Back on Track." *Auerbach,* 1997 (41-10-25).

Kliem, Ralph L., and Harris B. Anderson. "Teambuilding Styles and Their

Impact on Project Management Results." *Project Management Journal,* March 1996.

Kliem, Ralph L., and Rick Doughty. "Making Software Engineering Project Managers Successful." *Journal of Systems Management,* September 1987.

Klicm, Ralph L., and Jim L. Huie. "Evaluating Controls in a System Under Development." *Auerbach,* 1995 (73-10-10).

Kliem, Ralph L., and Irwin S. Ludin. "And Just-In-Time." *Journal of Systems Management,* November/December 1995.

———. "Developing a Project Management Methodology for IS Environments." *Managing System Development,* May 1996.

———. "Evaluating Project Performance." *Auerbach,* 1996 (35-10-60).

Knapp, Ellen. "How to Keep Knowledge Management from Flickering Out." *Computerworld (Leadership Series),* March 17, 1997.

Knutson, Joan. "Proposal Management: Generating Winning Proposals, Part 2." *PM Network,* March 1996.

Koch, Christopher. "Enter the Power Elite." *CIO,* May 1, 1996.

———. "The Bright Stuff." *CIO,* March 15, 1996.

Kramer, Matt. "Two Schedulers Streamline Chore of Setting Up Meetings." *PC Week,* May 8, 1995.

Laabs, Jennifer J. "Does Image Matter?" *Personnel Journal,* December 1995.

LaMonica, Martin. "Rumor keeps IS Shops Abreast of Project Development Risks." *InfoWorld,* October 23, 1995.

LaPlante, Alice. "Sharing the Wisdom." *Computerworld,* June 2, 1997.

Latham, John R. "Visioning: The Concept, Trilogy, and Process." *Quality Progress,* April 1995.

Lawton, George. "Project Management Comes to the Internet." *Software Magazine,* April 1997.

Leitch, John, Gerard Burke, Dom Nieves, Michael Little, and Michael Gorin. "Strategies for Involving Employees." *Journal for Quality and Participation,* September 1995.

Levine, Harvey A. "Risk Management for Dummies, Part 2." *PM Network,* April 1996.

———. "Risk Management for Dummies: Managing Schedule, Cost and Technical Risk and Contingency." *PM Network,* October 1995.

Linden, Robert C., Sandy J. Wayne, and Lisa Bradway. "Connections Make the Difference." *HR Magazine,* February 1996.

Lynch, Dina. "Unresolved Conflicts Affect the Bottomline." *HR Magazine,* May 1997.

MacKey, Wayne A., and John C. Carter. "Measure the Steps to Success." *IEEE Spectrum,* June 1994.

Macomber, John D. "You Can Manage Construction Risks." *Harvard Business Review,* March-April 1989.

Maglitta, Joseph. "Learning Lessons from IRS' Biggest Mistakes." *Computerworld,* October 14, 1996.

Maguire, Steve. "Leading a New Team." *Software Development,* May 1997.

Malloy, Amy. "Counting the Intangibles." *Computerworld,* June 1996.

Martin, James. "The Enterprise Engineer." *Computerworld (Leadership Series),* September 18, 1995.

McCarthy, Jim. "Better Teamwork." *Software Development,* December 1995.

McCune, Jenny C. "Guarding Your Software and Your Company." *Beyond Computing,* June 1997.

McGee, Marianne K. "Burnout." *Information Week,* March 4, 1996.

———. "Getting Credit for Your Career." *Information Week,* June 5, 1995.

———. "Outsourcing: Piecemeal Ticket." *Information Week,* July 14, 1997.

McGuinness, Charles. "Web Enabled Applications: Beyond Document Sharing." *Software Development,* February 1997.

Melymuka, Kathleen. "The Vision Thing." *Computerworld,* December 12, 1994.

———. "Virtual." *Computerworld,* April 28, 1997.

———. "Hell According to Yourdon." *Computerworld,* March 31, 1997.

Menagh, Melanie. "Virtues and Vices of the Virtual Corporation." *Computerworld,* November 13, 1995.

Menda, Kathleen. "Projects, Not Structure, Define Future Workplace." *HR Magazine,* March 1996.

Milas, Gene. "How to Develop a Meaningful Employee Recognition Program." *Quality Progress,* May 1995.

Minkiewicz, Arlene. "Objective Measures." *Software Development,* June 1997.

Mintzberg, Henry. "The Manager's Job: Folklore and Fact." *Harvard Business Review,* March-April 1990.

Moran, John W., and Glen D. Hoffherr. "Breakthrough Thinking." *Journal for Quality and Participation,* September 1995.

Myers, Marc. "Enterprise Project Management—It Can Be Automated." *Network World,* May 20, 1996.

Nakakoji, Kumiyo. "Beyond Language Translation: Crossing the Cultural Divide." *IEEE Software,* November 1996.

Narney, Chris. "Searching for True Knowledge." *Network World,* June 16, 1997.

Nelson, Bob, Lacl Good, and Tom Hill. "You Want Tomaytoes, I Want Tomahtoes." *Training,* June 1997.

Nixon, Kenneth L. "Management versus Teams." *The Quality Observer,* December 1995.

Nunn, Philip. "The Transition to Project Management in Manufacturing." *PM Network,* January 1995.

O'Connell, Sandra E. "The Virtual Workplace Moves At Warp Speed." *HR Magazine,* March 1996.

Pachter, Barbara. "Manners Matter." *Voyageur,* 1996.

————. "Six Keys to Writing Better Business Letters." *WFL,* May 1996.

Panepinto, Joe. "Maximize Teamwork." *Computerworld,* March 21, 1994.

Parr, William C., and Cheryl Hild. "Maintaining Focus Within Your Organization." *Quality Progress,* September 1995.

Paul, Lauren G. "User Input: Key to Avoiding Failure in Client/Server Development Projects." *PC Week,* January 25, 1995.

Pinto, Jeffrey. "Power and Politics: Managerial Implications." *PM Network,* August 1996.

Powell, David. "Group Communication." *Communications of the ACM,* April 1996.

Prencipe, Loretta. "It Takes Calm to Diffuse Anger." *Network World,* March 17, 1997.

Putnam, Lawrence H., Jr. "Using SEI Core Metrics." *Application Development Trends,* February 1995.

Racko, Roland. "Debugging Meetings." *Software Development,* September 1997.

Radosevich, Lynda, and Cheryl Dahle. "Taking Your Chances." *CIO,* April 15, 1996.

Richards, Dick. "A Perspective for Visionaries." *Journal for Quality and Participation,* September 1995.

Rieciardi, Philip. "Simplifying Your Approach to Measuring Performance." *Quality Digest,* August 1995.

Rifkin, Glenn. "Leadership: Can It Be Learned?" *Forbes ASAP,* April 8, 1996.

Roger, Will. "Slow Road to Copyright Legislation." *Interactive Week,* July 21, 1997.

Rose, Kenneth H. "A Performance Measurement Model." *Quality Progress,* February 1995.

Rubach, Laura. "Downsizing: How Quality Is Affected As Companies Shrink." *Quality Progress,* April 1995.

Rubin, Howard A. "Measurement Despite Its Promise, Successful Programs Are Rare." *Application Development Trends,* January 1995.

Runcie, John F. "The Ten Commandments of Leadership." *Journal for Quality and Participation,* October/November 1995.

Runge, Larry. "Starting from Scratch." *Computerworld,* October 24, 1994.

Saia, Rick. "Harvesting Project Leaders." *Computerworld,* July 21, 1997.

Sauder, Lew. "Team Players." *AS/400 Systems Management,* February 1997.

Saunders, Gary. "Mapping Administrative Processes." *Quality Digest,* August 1995.

Schatz, Willie. "The Burnout Syndrome." *Client/Server Journal,* August 1995.

————. "The Making of a Proper Project Manager." *Client/Server Journal,* October 1995.

Scheier, Robert L. "Businesses Outsourcing More, But Less Thrilled With Results." *Computerworld,* July 21, 1997.

Schlosberg, Jeremy. "Learning to Lead." *Computerworld,* September 9, 1996.

Schubert, Kathy. "So You've Been Asked to Be a Team Leader." *Journal for Quality and Participation,* September 1995.

Schultz, Beth. "A Real Virtual Network Corporation." *Network World,* January/February 1996.

————. "Collaboration by Design." *Network World,* January/February 1996.

Scully, John P. "People: The Imperfect Communicators." *Quality Progress,* April 1995.

Seadle, Michael. "Checkmating the Big Project Syndrome." *Enterprise Systems Journal,* April 1996.

Seesing, Paul R. "Distributing Project Control Database Information on the World Wide Web." *PM Network,* October 1996.

Seymour, Patricia. "Integration of Process Tools Key to Advanced A/D." *Application Development Trends,* February 1995.

Shacklett, Mary E. "Computerizing the Home-Based Work Force." *Enterprise Systems Journal,* July 1997.

Sherman, Strat. "Stretch Goals: The Dark Side of Asking for Miracles." *Fortune,* November 13, 1995.

Sims, Oliver. "Why Projects Don't Get Off to a Good Start." *Object Magazine,* October 1996.

Smith, Jim. "A Model for Ongoing Project Cost-Justification." *Network World,* February 5, 1996.

————. "Don't Look—The Project May Be Doomed." *Systems Management,* July 1995.

Smith, Max B. "Project Management of Outsourcing and Other Service Projects." *PM Network,* October 1996.

Smolens, Peter. "Mapping Out the Project Approval Process." *Network World,* November 25, 1996.

Sorgenfrei, Matt. "Separating the Wheat from the Chaff." *AS/400 Systems Management,* January 1997.

Sparrius, Ad. "You Can't Manage What You Don't Understand." *Project Management Journal* (reprint), March 1994.

Stamps, David. "Lights! Camera! Project Management." *Training,* January 1997.

Stein, Tom. "It Stalls at Xerox, Perrier." *Information Week,* March 31, 1997.

Stewart, Thomas A. "Planning a Career." *Fortune,* March 20, 1995.

Stokes, Stewart L., Jr. "Rewards and Recognition for Teams." *Information Systems Management,* Summer 1995.

Stone, John A. "How to Keep Control of Big Development Projects." *Information Week,* September 16, 1996.

Stua.t, Anne. "The Adaptable Workforce." *CEO,* March 1, 1995.

Sullivan, John, and Dave Yesua. "The Internet: Faster, Better, Riskier." *PM Network,* October 1996.

Sullivan, Kristina B. "Group Schedulers Run Gamut." *PC Week,* November 29, 1993.

Surveyer, Jacques. "A Project Aide on CD-ROM." *Information Week,* February 12, 1996.

————. "Project Management Tools." *Software Development,* July 1997.

Tapscott, Don. "Leadership for the Internetworked Business." *Information Week,* November 13, 1995.

Tate, Priscilla. "Endangered Species: Project Methodologies." *Client/Server Journal,* October 1995.

Teal, Thomas. "The Human Side of Management." *Harvard Business Review,* November-December 1996.

The, Lee. "How to Hire a Consultant." *Datamation,* February 15, 1996.

———. "IS-Friendly Project Management." *Datamation,* April 1, 1996.

Toney, Frank. "Good Results Yield . . . Resistance?" *PM Network,* October 1996.

———. "What the Fortune 500 Know About PM Best Practices." *PM Network,* February 1997.

Venick, Martin. "Managing Distributed Projects with Panache." *Client/Server Journal,* February 1996.

Venturato, Anthony P. "Consultants: Judging the Potential for Excellence." *PM Network,* March 1997.

Wallace, Bob. "Using the Internet for Project Management." *Computerworld,* October 14, 1996.

Walsh, Jeff. "Primavera, Microsoft to Face Off on Project Management." *InfoWorld,* June 2, 1997.

Wang, Jim, and Ron Watson. "Five Keys to Making Your OO Project Succeed." *Object Magazine,* November 1996.

Weissman, Steve. "The Push and Pull of Getting Project Approval." *Network World,* October 23, 1995.

Weitz, Lori. "New Features, Ease of Use Expanding Project Management Base." *Client/Server Computing,* January 1994.

Weldon, David. "Living on Shaky Ground." *Computerworld,* February 5, 1996.

———. "A Mutual Understanding." *Computerworld,* May 1, 1995.

Wells, Jess. "Painless Dismissals." *Software Development,* May 1997.

Whitaker, Ken. "Managing Software Maniacs." *Computerworld,* January 9, 1995.

White, Randall P. "Seekers and Scalers: The Future Leaders." *Training and Development,* January 1997.

Wiegers, Karl. "Metrics: 10 Trap to Avoid." *Software Development,* October 1997.

Wigglesworth, David C. "Assess White-Collar Skills in the New Economy." *HR Magazine,* May 1996.

Wilde, Candee. "The Limits of Power." *Computerworld,* January 16, 1995.

Williamson, Mickey. "Getting a Grip on Groupware." *CIO,* Mrach 1, 1996.

Wilson, Linda. "SWAT Teams: Life on the Edge." *Computerworld,* October 23, 1995.

Wolleat, J. R. "Helluva Project." *Computerworld,* November 18, 1996.

Wood, Lamont. "Perfect Harmony." *Information Week,* May 8, 1995.

Wyatt, Robert. "How to Assess Risk." *Systems Management,* October 1995.

Yeack, William, and Leonard Sayles. "Virtual and Real Organizations: Optimal Paring." *PM Network,* August 1996.

Yourdon, Ed. "Surviving a Death March." *Software Development,* July 1997.

Zawrotny, Stan. "Demystifying the Black Art of Project Estimating." *Application Development Trends,* July 1995.

Index